"In *This Is ActionBrand Marketing*, seasoned marketing strategist Mark Imperial demystifies the intricate dance between branding and marketing. With his sharp insights and straightforward approach, Mark unveils the often misunderstood relationship between these two critical components of business success. This book is a game-changer for entrepreneurs, business owners, and professionals seeking clarity and direction in the often chaotic world of marketing and branding.

Mark doesn't just theorize; he brings decades of in-the-trenches experience, guiding thousands of entrepreneurs from various fields. His book is not just informative; it's a practical guide that addresses common frustrations and questions, providing actionable solutions and a clear path to business growth and brand development. Imperial covers everything from developing a strong brand identity to leveraging social media effectively. His unique approach, focusing on ActionBrand Marketing, empowers readers to build their brand as a byproduct of cash flow from immediate sales, a strategy as innovative as it is effective.

This book is a must-read for business owners or entrepreneurs who are serious about making a mark in the competitive business world. It's a blueprint for success, offering strategies that are trackable and reliable and designed to set you apart in a crowded market."

- Mike Capuzzi
  www.MikeCapuzzi.com

"I've known Mark for over 15 years, and he's always been a straight-to-the-point, no-nonsense guy - and a brilliant marketer. That is extremely evident throughout this power-packed masterpiece, where he delivers a comprehensive, non-stop firehose of actionable business-building strategies that add up to a fool-proof business-building system. You will want to keep this book right next to your desk and refer to it again and again."

- Steve Sipress, Creator of The WOW! Strategy™ SmallBusiness Success Program
  www.TheWOWStrategy.com

"This book lays it all out when it comes to marketing. I know many who have spent thousands of dollars to learn what is in Mark's book. I've had the opportunity to see Mark in action. When it comes to marketing, he knows what he's talking about. Mark isn't just teaching you; he has walked the walk, making him my favorite kind of author. I've been doing this for a long time, and I learn from Mark. He's sharing what he has used and succeeded with for his business and what has worked for his clients. Talk about value."

- Dan Cricks
  Results Marketing
  GreatResultsMarketing.com

"Mark's book offers a refreshing perspective on the critical relationship between marketing and branding, emphasizing the essential role of marketing in building a successful brand. With plenty of practical insights and a unified approach, this book provides excellent guidance for seasoned professionals and aspiring entrepreneurs. This book is a must-read for anyone looking to achieve predictable growth and revenues within their business."

- Craig Valine, Business Growth Strategist

"Mark Imperial has created a masterful combination of direct response marketing and strategic branding with his ActionBrand Marketing methodology. I've known Mark for over 20 years. As a fellow independent business advisor trained by the legendary Dan Kennedy, I can attest firsthand that Mark is an excellent marketer who has helped business owners build their brands and businesses. In this book, he lays out a clear blueprint for attracting high-quality leads, boosting conversions, and gaining market dominance through the combined powers of irresistible offers and memorable brand-building. This is not just theory – Mark provides concrete, tactical advice that any business owner or marketer can immediately implement for rapid, sustainable growth and profitability. Any business owner or entrepreneur will gain insights from this book and grow their business just by implementing a few of the techniques he lays out in his blueprint."

- Becky Auer, CEO of No BS Marketing & Instant Impact Media
www.BeckyAuer.com

"If you own a business - this is a must-read. ActionBrand - broken down, will change the business forever. Great book, simple read, and actionable steps lead to a touchdown!"

- Richelle Shaw, Author of Million Dollar Partnerships

THIS IS
ACTIONBRAND
MARKETING

THE UNIFIED BRANDING AND DIRECT RESPONSE SYSTEM FOR ACCELERATING PROFITS AND WINNING HEARTS

MARK IMPERIAL

This Is ActionBrand Marketing/ Mark Imperial -- 1st ed.
Chief Editor/ Shannon Buritz

ISBN: 978-1-954757-42-4

The Publisher has strived to be as accurate and complete as possible in the creation of this book.

This book is not intended for use as a legal, business, accounting, or financial advice source. All readers are advised to seek the services of competent professionals in legal, business, accounting, and finance fields.

Like anything else in life, there are no guarantees of income or results in practical advice books. Readers are cautioned to rely on their judgment about their individual circumstances to act accordingly.

While all attempts have been made to verify information provided in this publication, the Publisher assumes no responsibility for errors, omissions, or contrary interpretation of the subject matter herein. Any perceived slights of specific persons, peoples, or organizations are unintentional.

This book is dedicated to my beautiful bride, Shannon.
Everything we set our minds to turns to gold.
The universe wants us together; it is inevitable.

Contents

Acknowledgments

"In learning you will teach, and in teaching you will learn."

PHIL COLLINS

This book exists because I became addicted to marketing and branding. Dan Kennedy showed me marketing when it wasn't even marketing that I thought I needed.

In the '80s and '90s, I was a DJ and one of the pioneers of the Chicago House music scene. One of my DJ club jobs was spinning music for the late great Walter Payton's string of Chicagoland nightclubs, which led me to branch out with my own DJ service.

Mark with the late great Walter Payton
at the Pacific Club in Lombard, Illinois

When I thought my DJ company needed another gimmick, an-other follow-along dance, another product or service to sell (if we ever meet in person, ask me about the "Glowbot" folly), it was actually something else that I needed.

We needed to show the world we existed, and the missing piece was marketing.

Once I discovered marketing, my business skyrocketed, going from an empty calendar to booked solid in less than six months. I figured out how to turn on profits like a faucet!

My DJ business led me to become the experiential marketing voice for some of the world's most famous and loved brands, including Nintendo, Pokemon, and Under Armour, to name a few. This experience is where I learned how branding works for the big brands to bring it to small businesses, too.

I've come to realize that a remarkable set of circumstances has led to my passion for branding and marketing. First, I'm from Chicago, the birthplace of advertising. Legendary names in advertising like Albert Lasker, Leo Burnett, Lord & Thomas, and Claude Hopkins came from this city known as the nation's advertising commercial capital. Ronald McDonald, Tony the Tiger, Snap, Crackle, & Pop, the Jolly Green Giant, Mr. Clean, Charlie Tuna, and the Pillsbury Dough Boy were all created in Chicago.

I've had the honor to create and implement experiential marketing events for brands here like McDonald's, M&M's, Masterfoods, Milky Way, Snickers, and Dove Bar, among others. I was working in branding before I learned direct response marketing.

Mark hosting the Pokémon World Championships in Hawaii

While I was growing my DJ business the hard way and becoming successful despite myself, I accidentally discovered Dan Kennedy, known for his genius in direct response marketing, when a friend of mine asked me to accompany him to a mega-seminar called Success 1996 held by Peter Lowe at the United Center here in Chicago. Dan was the last speaker nobody heard of, but his message had the most significant impact because it was no BS and actionable information minus the feel-good motivational talk. Every investment I made applying what I learned from Dan measurably grew my DJ business, and for the first time, I felt in control. Naturally, I got certified by Dan in 2008, ran his Chicago SW chapter through 2016, and wrote the "Grow Your Local Business Column" in Dan's newsletter for three years, reaching 26K+ subscribers.

This made me more in demand with the big brands because I was then the "odd duck," bringing direct response headlines and attention-grabbing words to my experiential branding work. I know how to use direct response and branding together, resulting in this book.

Mark with Dan Kennedy for his No BS Independent Business Advisor certification in 2008

Besides a branding and marketing addict, I'm a DJ, a disc jockey, and a remixer. I curate and remix music selections in the most elegant, orchestrated way, designed to touch your emotions. I could whip you up into a dancing frenzy if that is what I want to accomplish, or I can mellow you out for an ultimate chill vibe.

The notes were already there before Mozart came along. Same with marketing and branding. The principles were already established. I merely curated and remixed them into a new adaptation. At heart, I'm a curator. We all are curators. I may have invented the methodology of **"ActionBrand Marketing"**; however, it is a curation (as all systems are), an arrangement, a choreography, a proprietary unification of branding and direct response marketing. It is the most elegant way I have found to drive sales and profits while simultaneously building a brand, leading to a flywheel of insane, contagious growth.

While Dan Kennedy started my quenchless thirst for marketing knowledge as a direct mentor, there are many other gurus from whom I have gleaned brilliant insights, either from working with them, hiring them, joining their programs, or learning from their trainings.

I want to acknowledge the following experts and thank them for their insights:

Dan S. Kennedy
Bill Glazer
Russell Brunson
Gary Halbert
Jay Abraham
Chet Holmes
Perry Marshall

Ryan Deiss

Perry Belcher

Jim Edwards

Mike Stewart

Mike Koenigs

Joe Polish

Dave Dee

Jack Mize

Brian Horn

Bob Regnerus

Stewart Andrew Alexander

Darin Spindler

Mark Imperial and Perry Marshall in Chicago

Because I fell in love with marketing and branding, I'm proud to memorialize my magic method in this book. ActionBrand Marketing is the fastest path for any business to go from stuck to thriving, using the simple unified system of direct response marketing and branding working harmoniously together. This has never been done in a single book before. Help more people with your business, profit wildly, repeat!

Introduction

Interesting fact: Marketing works without branding; however, branding doesn't work without marketing. This will become clear inside this book. Too many businesses fail to succeed due to a lack of understanding of the relationship between marketing and branding, and it doesn't have to be that way. Business owners and self-employed professionals have been misguided or not guided at all, and it's not their fault.

When people dream of working for themselves or owning a business, often the ideas of how to get a client or a customer and how to run a business if they choose to start one are afterthoughts, so many find themselves behind the eightball once they open their doors and hang out their shingle.

To make things worse, they don't teach you how to build a brand or market your business or whether one action is more important. I'll say one thing now that will set the tone for this book, and it will become more apparent as we go along, and that is...

"You don't build a brand to get a customer. You get a customer to build a brand."

Branding and marketing are both important; until now, they've been treated as separate subjects. This book aims to show you an optimized and unified system that accomplishes both in the most effective order and doses.

This book is for you if...

1. You already own a business and are either dissatisfied with your progress or are eager for a better system for growth.

    OR

2. You're starting a new business or professional practice and want the most effective, efficient, and repeatable marketing plan that gives you the quickest path to predictable revenue and growth. Perhaps the pandemic inspired you to join "The Great Resignation" and finally build something of your own.

    OR

3. You're a seasoned branding or marketing professional who gets value from seeing fresh perspectives. You may already know everything about the subjects, and much of this may be a review. However, you value reviewing the fundamentals, seeing a new curated system, and knowing that school is never out for the true professional.

Butcher, baker, or candlestick maker. Attorney, financial advisor, or dog groomer. People build businesses they believe they will enjoy. Or they build businesses they think will bring them wealth. They go to school, get degrees, and get certifications to become good at what they want to do. There is a misconception that their certification or education will guarantee success, and it just isn't enough.

Unfortunately, more than one business owner I have interviewed told me that in all the years of their education and training, not one day was spent on being taught how to get a client or customer. That's very alarming because without the capabilities of attracting prospects and selling them into becoming clients or customers, no amount of good service matters. Nothing happens until someone sells something, and new business owners are sent off into the world woefully unprepared. Marketing and selling are other skill sets altogether. You could even call them a second career.

You are an expert at your craft. You are great at what you do and serving your customers and clients. In most cases, whatever profession you studied or whatever educational degree you accomplished, they likely didn't spend enough time teaching you how to get a customer or client. Or, they didn't spend one day teaching you marketing or sales because perhaps they assumed everyone would be working for someone else. You believed you would be armed with everything you needed to be successful. Unfortunately, if they didn't teach you marketing, advertising, or sales, they did you a disservice.

Another challenge is that you may have been sold and tried other marketing or advertising methods that didn't work for you. You probably didn't have the right guide or a tell-all book like this to show you the way. Don't worry; this book will give you principles that reveal why those past methods may not have worked and what to do instead.

Predatory salespeople try to sell you "their" solution, whether it suits your circumstances or not. This book will shed light on what works in specific situations so you can make more informed choices.

Once you learn the principles of effective and efficient client/customer-getting, you'll be able to just say "No!" to the salespeople trying to take your money.

The good news is that you are a whisper away from all the success you want because just one simple ActionBrand Marketing campaign is all you need to get started toward a life of freedom, wealth, and autonomy, and you're about to see what that looks like.

If you want better business growth, you probably have questions such as...

"How can I develop a strong brand identity?"
"What are the most effective advertising strategies for my business?"
"What's the quickest way to start making sales in my business?"
"How can I improve my online presence?"
"How do I make my business stand out from the crowd?"
"What's the best way to use social media for business growth?"
"Where should I begin marketing my business if I'm tight on time and budget?"

Have you ever felt these frustrations?

"A salesperson sold me an advertisement, which didn't work!"
"I know half of my marketing isn't working; I just don't know which half!"
"I'm posting on all the social platforms like I've been told, and nothing is happening!"
"The competition is driving our prices down, and all people ask is how much I charge!"

Don't worry; you're not alone. This book will answer those questions and more. Plus, it will give you the solution to end those frustrations once and for all.

In this book, you'll discover...

- A simple, proven system for simultaneously building your brand for free as a byproduct of cash flow from immediate sales.
- The smart way to use social media for exponential reach and to grow your prospect list fast.
- The DNA method for standing out from your competition, so you are seen as the obvious expert and choice.
- How to control your own media to reduce your dependence on expensive ads.
- How to ensure all of your marketing is trackable, so you know it is working.
- The Trust Triggers that create sales fastest.
- Your Prime Positioning Portfolio: The foundational marketing assets you need to gain clients and customers fastest.
- Your Nucleus Marketing Tool that everything orbits around.
- The Profit Loops you can optimize and trigger at will.
- Symbiotic Marketing methods that grow your referral partner network.
- ...and much more.

Starting, growing, and scaling a business or professional practice can be overwhelming. But it doesn't have to be. In the sport of Boxing, there are only six basic strikes to master. Mastery in Boxing is about chaining those strikes into effective combinations with grace, speed, and timing, flowing with your opponent's moves! In marketing your business, hundreds or thousands of tactics may appear like shiny objects; however, you only need to master a few fundamentals, which you will brilliantly whip into multiple profitable combinations, flowing with the conditions of your market!

With three decades of in-the-trenches experience, I've personally guided more than 6,000 entrepreneurs in marketing their businesses ranging from inception to seven figures and reached tens of thousands more through media, leveraging my experience as a seasoned experiential marketer and voice for globally acclaimed brands like Nintendo, M&M/Mars Candy and UnderArmour, to name a few.

I've seen many people make costly mistakes and waste a ton of time trying random acts of marketing, which could have easily been avoided if they just implemented the proper fundamentals and a clear action plan.

I wrote this book to give you a solid action plan for growing and scaling your business or professional practice or starting a brand new business using the client/customer-getting power of ActionBrand Marketing.

Let me be clear. While this book is packed with valuable information about ActionBrand Marketing your business, there are many ways to be correct. There is no single right answer for everyone, but this system will serve as a proven, reliable foundation that can provide rapid, dramatic growth.

Even though the differences may be small, every situation is unique. So, if you have a question or concern not addressed in this book, I'm here to help. You can reach my team and me for a complimentary Action Plan Session at www.markimperial.com or email us at actionplan@markimperial.com.

To your success!
MARK IMPERIAL

How to Avoid the Eight Biggest Branding and Marketing Traps

Marketing is vital. It shouldn't be taken lightly. In fact, it should be treated as a higher priority than your core service or product quality. This chapter will reveal what's wrong with most marketing and what to do to ensure you don't get caught by any of these common branding and marketing traps.

The SBA (Small Business Administration) reported the top five causes of business failure in Forbes magazine:

1. No market need
2. Not enough capital
3. Not the right team
4. Competition
5. Pricing

Speaking of pricing, I recall an "I Love Lucy" episode titled "The Million Dollar Idea." Lucy and Ethel go into business producing Aunt Martha's salad dressing recipe. Lucy offered the punch line, "Maybe there's no profit on each salad dressing jar, but we'll make it up in volume." Unfortunately, a business owner with this mindset is no laughing matter.

Studies show that 90% of all small business startups fail. That is a scary statistic.

It doesn't have to be this way. In many cases, improper marketing is the only thing preventing success if there is a demand for a product or service. I wrote this book to give you a better system and to show you what it takes to succeed. I want to bring awareness to this problem and give you a solid, actionable plan to get as many clients, patients, or customers as you wish, predictably and profitably.

Marketing Failure Is Not Your Fault

No matter what service you provide or professional practice you are in, you probably spent a significant amount of time getting degrees, certifications, or ongoing education. However, from what I've heard from many of my clients who come to me for a marketing autopsy, most of these courses don't spend one day teaching you how to get a client, patient, or customer. Client acquisition is an afterthought in these courses. They focus on teaching you how to do your job well, which is essential; however, the public has no benchmark on how good you are until someone hires you. Herein lies the problem. It is always a shame when I see a "Going Out of Business" ad being the first effective ad from a company just because they'd never been taught. Perhaps it is assumed you will go out and get a job at a company that already has the marketing and advertising figured out. But either way, your instructors have done you a disservice, and they're ultimately letting you down.

The Eight Biggest Branding and Marketing Traps

People make eight common mistakes when attempting to market their businesses. Let's discuss each one.

Trap #1: Copying Advertising or Marketing Blindly

Since we are all inundated with commercials and ads daily, we assume they should be easy to create. But creating effective ads is an entire craft of psychology and other concepts that are rarely taught. Sometimes the familiar translates to having a false sense of expert knowledge. For example, people often think they have a good grasp of real estate just because they have lived in a house or an apartment their entire lives. Any realtor will tell you there's more to it than that. Similarly, if you are an avid restaurant-goer, you might think you have "seen it all" and that running a restaurant would be a piece of cake. But you will find that this is more challenging than it seems.

Another example of blind copying is when people go into business; they look around at what others in the field are doing to promote their company and try to replicate it. Legendary success author Earl Nightingale once stated, "If you have no known successful model to follow, look around at what everyone else is doing and do the opposite. The majority is always wrong." He emphasized that only 5% of the population in any field is successful, and many are copying the 95% who are barely getting by. Conformity can be a problem.

Trap #2: Copying a Lead-Generation Ad

Lead-generation ads don't necessarily make money; they're meant to generate leads. The ad itself could be losing money on the front end. In other words, you spend money to acquire the names, contact information, or responses, but you may not *make* any money on those items. These names and contacts are being generated at a loss only to recover costs through other ways, such as promotions and higher-priced offers beneath the surface.

Another big secret is that lead generation companies rent the lists they've created. Let's look at an example. We have all seen the ads in magazines for check printing, where you can have puppies or city skylines printed on your personal checks for dirt cheap. Secretly, these are giant lead generation companies. This was a mindblowing discovery for me. When you order a set of checks from them, they aren't making any money, breaking even on printing costs. However, they now have your name and contact information and know that you like puppies. This information goes into a database, and the list becomes available on the list rental market, a behind-the-scenes secret society of advertisers seeking out direct mail professionals and list brokers. There is a giant catalog of lists in this underground market.

So how's that for fascinating? You need to understand the type of ad you are trying to copy because things aren't always what they appear.

Trap #3: Copying a Loss Leader Ad

A loss leader ad loses money every time it runs. A preconceived notion exists that it must be making money because you always see the commercial. However, the truth is that money is lost each time a new customer is generated. Remember infomercials promoting a book for $19.95 or even $39.95? You might think profits are made on book sales, but the reality is that they are likely losing money or barely breaking even on the cost of running the ad. Authors who think they will get rich by writing a book often don't understand where the money really comes from. Similar to the lead generation example, something beneath the surface will be offered or sold to create a return on investment. Often, a book is a way to capture a lead so they can be sold a high-priced investment in more education, a product, or any other high-ticket slack adjuster. When we look at a guru selling their book, a backend example could be selling a $5,000 to $10,000 coaching program, online course, or done-for-you service.

A loss leader example of a physical product is Proactiv Skin Care by Guthy-Renker. Perhaps they sell the first tube of acne "glop" for $29. It was reported several years ago that when Proactiv divided their ad spend by how many orders they received, it was costing them $100 to $150 to acquire a customer who was only paying $29 for their bottle of glop. So they are always in the negative while running their commercials. But they do know their numbers, and if the average person keeps putting the glop on their face for X number of months, they are hitting profits perhaps six months later.

So, what does this do? My mentor, Dan Kennedy, popularized the expression, "He who can spend the most money to generate a customer wins." Proactiv has been in the business long, so they know how to make tons of money with that model. And this thwarts the competition because people may blindly copy their ad, thinking they can compete alongside Guthy-Renker. But, they will quickly find themselves in trouble, especially if they are not as well-funded.

Before you create a loss leader ad, you need to test it and look at your numbers and baseline. You must know what the value of that customer will be on average through subsequent purchases or subscriptions over some time. Then, you can determine the sustainability of that ad. Test it with a reasonable amount of money you are willing to risk, and then roll it out slowly.

Trap #4: Copying Already-Established Brands

This is a common mistake because, again, we all watch TV. And since we can recite infomercials word for word, we think that qualifies us as marketing and advertising geniuses. But if you are not astute about the principles, you could make a massive mistake by copying an already-established brand.

Established brands have spent decades or even a hundred years and millions or billions of dollars to become consumer household names. For example, everyone knows what Coca-Cola is. All an ad has to do is say, "Coke is the real thing," and it triggers your memory because you are already familiar with it, which is an awareness campaign. They have the luxury of doing silly ads that don't sell or promote their product. Super Bowl commercials are an excellent example of this. And these ads are costly. But a company like Coca-Cola can afford to run them. Just "showing up" is enough to keep people coming back for the product. Even more, the ads are really aimed at the retailers, driving distribution to ensure retailers keep stocking their items. But if you're a solo practitioner or a small business owner who needs to make a living, you probably don't have the deep pockets to spend millions of dollars on awareness.

Let's look at a company like De Beers ("A diamond is forever."). De Beers and one ad agency are almost entirely responsible for the universal acceptance of the idea that dating and courtship should end with a marriage proposal and a diamond engagement ring. The concept of a diamond ring symbolizing engagement hasn't been around as long as everyone thinks. It became the norm in the late 1940s, right after De Beers poured on the marketing dollars, started running campaigns, and created awareness to indicate that diamonds were the only respectable way to propose to your partner. If you look back at history, the ancient Romans simply used gold bands. But there was only a de facto standard once De Beers decided it was diamonds. It just so happened that De Beers came upon a surplus of diamonds in Africa. They built diamond mines and artificially created demand and scarcity to increase prices. And it worked.

Now, if you were to open a diamond store, you would benefit from the billions of dollars of advertising De Beer poured into the marketplace over decades. The more significant part of this lesson is that De Beers had deep pockets and reported spending upwards of $10 million yearly on advertising campaigns. That was a lot of money back in the 40s. But they were promoting and marketing an idea, not directly a product. They weren't the only company selling diamonds but the only company advocating for diamonds in marriage proposals. So they essentially created an entire industry for themselves and their competitors. But the key thing to remember is this was a deep pockets game.

Trap #5: Imitating Meaningless Taglines

You are likely familiar with Nike's slogan of "Just Do It." Or Capital One's question, "What's in your wallet?" Those might sound clever. But again, companies like Nike have spent billions of dollars over many decades drilling those taglines into our brains. So they are reaping the benefits after much ad spend. That's what big brands do. So we "ActionBranders" will do things a little bit differently.

If you were brand new to the marketplace and had never heard of Nike, the tagline "Just Do It" would mean diddly squat and not drive any sales or business action whatsoever. Every time I turn on the TV, I'm asked, "What's in your wallet?" during at least one commercial break. Will Capital One benefit over time? Maybe. Is it a deep pockets game? Most definitely. Is it practical for small business owners or independent service professionals?

Probably not the wisest path. Is creating a catchy tagline totally useless? The short answer is no. In the chapter about the DNA of an ActionBrand, you'll discover what to do instead. Slogans and taglines should take a backseat to clarity, a clear message. For now, understand that a tagline like "Just Do It" or "What's in your wallet?" does absolutely nothing to drive sales until you invest what it takes to anchor that slogan directly to you in the minds of your consumers. And that's an exercise that can cost millions of dollars and decades of time. ActionBrand Marketing will show you a smarter way.

Trap #6: Being a Victim of Sales Predators and Marketing Confusion

Everyone who has advertising space to sell needs business owners to buy their spaces. They often want to get "their thing" into your hands while diminishing others. It could be ad space in a magazine, the Yellow Pages, radio, or TV. You probably won't be attacked by direct mail, as I haven't seen any active sales reps for the United States Post Office. But that's the only one you don't have to worry about.

At the end of the day, who are these predators? They're salespeople. But are they marketing experts? I don't know if you can call them that. Some may have a little education, but they are selling ad space for the most part. And often, they greedily try to sell you their ad space by insulting or damaging others. Also, they tend to completely disregard whether or not their particular media or advertising vehicle is appropriate for your type of business. So this leads to a lot of confusion because business owners will often take the salespeople at face value, and they might even mistake them for marketing experts. I've seen this happen too often, damaging people's confidence in marketing and advertising altogether.

But unfortunately, marketing and advertising on their own aren't to blame. It is the poor use and misdirection of these methods causing the failure. So business owners get into the habit of saying, "Radio doesn't work. TV doesn't work. Valpak doesn't work." You can pretty much fill in the blank with anything. But was it the actual thing that didn't work? Or was it the improper use of the thing? I'm glad you picked up this book to gain clarity on those questions.

Trap #7: Marketing Noise

There is so much clutter out there trying to grab your prospect's attention; how will you stand out amongst all that noise? Forbes Magazine reported that people are exposed to 4,000 to 10,000 advertising messages daily.With the increasing number of platforms like TikTok and Instagram and the paid influencers "exposing" products and brands, this noise is accelerating at blinding speeds. So can you see how people fervently try to ignore as much as possible, shutting everything off, deleting emails, and throwing junk mail directly into the trash? They are simply trying to minimize the noise and distraction in their lives. So the significant challenge today is grabbing attention amid that noisy environment. We will solve that dilemma in the chapter about the DNA of an ActionBrand.

Trap #8: Bad Messaging

In a seminar for my DJ marketing students, I pulled up advertisements on the big screen of the most common ads in the industry for wedding DJs and entertainers.

The most common theme is that companies talk about themselves too much. I got through to these students by simply describing it as "these ads are designed to impress other DJs." Talking about the size of their music library, the wattage of their sound systems, and how many years they have been in business are things only other DJs would know or care about. A bride isn't looking for sound system specs; they want a successful celebration their family and friends will talk fondly about for years to come. No bride cares about a DJ until they know the DJ cares about them. In this book, you'll learn how to speak to the interest of your target market, so they are drawn to you.

My chief aim in writing this book is to help clarify and simplify your marketing and branding and help you avoid unnecessary complexity and confusion. The good news is that, although it's simple in principle and the word "easy" is hard to spell, I will give you greater clarity around branding and marketing your business effectively! In the next chapter, I will define some terms so we can dig in and better understand what works.

Terminology

Before we dive in further, let's get some terminology straight. If you're reading this, you may be an experienced marketer or a beginner. I won't assume too much. If you're an advanced marketer, you may skip this chapter because I will cover the basics here. On the other hand, even if you are an experienced marketer, you may enjoy this refresher.

What Is Marketing?

Let's start with the definition of "marketing." According to the AMA (American Marketing Association's) definition: "Marketing is the activity, set of institutions, and processes for creating, communicating, delivering, and exchanging offerings that have value for customers, clients, partners, and society at large." This was the AMA's most recent definition in 2017, and they have not updated it up to the time of this writing. But this is what I say about marketing: so many things can be considered part of marketing. Pretty much everything that you do can be called "marketing."

For instance, take a look at Disney World. Every night, they put a fresh coat of paint on the railings, the fences, and the garbage cans so they look brand new in the morning. After people visit Disney World, they tell their friends how brand new and fresh the park always looks, no matter when they go there. This activity that causes word of mouth can be considered marketing.

Take note of how Disney trains its whole crew, including the maintenance staff. If a guest were to ask the janitor a question, they could quickly answer and take on the role of a park guide. Marketing the theme park's features and highlighting the Disney experience is baked into all staffers' training.

Disney's holistic approach to enhancing customer experience highlights that anything that can be communicated can be turned into a marketing activity. Marketing includes appearance. Everything about Disney theme parks, from the fresh paint, clean premises, and staff uniforms, communicate the parks' value.

In short, marketing is anything that drives positive experiences. In turn, these experiences drive word of mouth. As you may clearly see, demonstrating benefits and positive experiences through marketing makes it work, regardless if "branding" is also being applied. More on this later.

What Is Advertising?

Often people will mention marketing and advertising as if they are the same thing. That's a common misconception. Advertising is only one small part of marketing. As I said in the marketing definition, any activity that grabs attention and draws attention to your business is considered marketing. You definitely do this with advertising.

According to the AMA, "Advertising is the placement of announcements and messages in time or space by business firms, nonprofit organizations, government agencies, and individuals who seek to inform and/or persuade members of a particular target market or audience regarding their products, services, organizations or ideas."

Examples of advertising include paid or unpaid ad placements in media. These can range from television commercials, radio commercials, print (display advertising is considered print), online advertising, and social media advertising — any media that has or offers advertising space.

What Is Promotion?

Promotions are typically event-driven. You'll often see in-store promotions of new brands, perhaps new soft drinks, and they're offering taste tests and samples. You can see this a lot at Costco. This is a form of promotion called "sampling." Other forms of promotion could be special events or public stunts choreographed, scheduled, and executed to bring attention and drive awareness and action to a specific company objective, from a product release to a special announcement.

Suppose the circus was coming to town, and they got a license from the city to walk the elephant through the downtown district with a sign on its back. This is considered a promotion or promotional stunt.

What Is Selling?

Selling happens when the activity of marketing brings a prospect in front of you who is interested in something that you have to offer. Selling is where interested candidates are educated about the product or service's benefits to make an informed decision to buy.

What Is a Brand?

According to the AMA, a brand is a "name, term, design, symbol, or any other feature that identifies one seller's goods or service as distinct from those of other sellers."

The ISO, or the International Organization for Standardization, defines "brand" as an "intangible asset intended to create distinctive images and associations in the minds of stakeholders, thereby generating economic benefit/values."

To get the core of the marketing power of a brand, we need to step back thousands of years into history. The practice of marking livestock with fire-heated iron in different shapes dates back to around 2700 BCE. Branding livestock is thought to have originated with the ancient Egyptians. The idea behind branding is that it protects livestock from theft since the villagers would come to know the specific shape of different farms' branding irons. They would eventually know which livestock belonged to which farm.

As things turned out, each farm would naturally develop a reputation for the quality of its livestock. People would begin to link farms' reputations with the shapes they marked on their animals. This association between ownership, reputation, and product marking became known as branding. This practice evolved over the years and carried branding over to other things besides livestock. Products, businesses, and even people are now being branded.

Today, the term "brand" encompasses the personality and reputation of a product, business, or person. The term "branding" refers to the act of distinguishing a company's product or a person from other competitors through different communication channels.

The Five Basic Elements of a Brand

1. Affinity

The first element of a brand is "affinity." Affinity refers to the target audience that the brand wants to sell to. You can quickly know if a business owner is a rookie by asking who their ideal customer is. The rookie will answer, "Anybody! Anybody can use my product." This is a big mistake because being nonspecific and vague will get you the least attention or response.

You must understand that the tighter you can identify with a particular person's situation or interests, whatever these may be, the more easily you'll get that person's attention. People like to buy and do business with companies and purchase products that they feel were truly made just for them.

2. Identity

The next essential element of a brand is "identity." This involves the look and feel of the company or the product. At the most basic level, identity is what most people associate with a brand. They think of a brand by its logo, color scheme, and font. They mistakenly assume that branding is only about this shallow, surface-level appearance.

This is one of the most common mistakes would-be entrepreneurs make when starting a business. They first think, "I have to have a logo." They feel that all you need is a logo to create a brand. In reality, a logo is only one tiny piece of a brand. Why? A logo has zero meaning until you give it meaning.

To build a strong brand, you want to maintain a consistent identity with your target audience so they can associate or "anchor" your company's name, performance, and reputation to your logo over time.

3. Brand Personality

The next foundational element is the "personality" of a brand. It is another big piece of a brand. It's the emotion that your brand conveys to your target market. What type of personality do you want to express in your brand? Does your company want to be taken seriously? Are you a casual company? Are you more fun-loving?

This is something that you need to carefully consider when crafting any piece of advertising or planning a promotion. Your brand personality will shine through when you adequately express yourself or your brand through your marketing messages.

4. Positioning

Where do you want your brand to stand in your field? Where do you want your brand to stand in the mind of your ideal audience? Do you want to be considered the high-end choice? Or are you the value-driven choice?

Carefully decide what level of value your target market will associate with your brand.

5. Statement of Values

The last brand element to consider is the brand's "statement of values." This acts as a brand's promise. Your brand's statement of values tells the world what you believe in.

Your statement of values answers the following questions: What values guide your company? Who do you stand for, and who do you stand against? Who do you defend? Who do you help? Who do you protect? And who and what do you protect them from?

Your statement of values lays out what your brand promises its customers. With this understanding, you can see that giving a product or service a "brand" or personality will do nothing without implementing "marketing" so the world can know it exists.

Now that we're clear on terminology, we can begin discussing how ActionBrand Marketing inextricably links marketing and branding for fast cash flow and accelerated growth.

Introducing the ActionBrand Marketing System: Could There Be One Marketing and Branding System Superior to All the Rest?

"Many paths lead from the foot of the mountain, but at the peak, we all gaze at the single bright moon."

IKKYU

Businesses waste colossal amounts of money on marketing and advertising that doesn't work. Anything can technically "work," but everything you do returns varying degrees of results. It's really up to you to decide what results are acceptable. And there are several factors to consider, such as the cost of attracting interested parties that you can nurture into sales.

There are paths to make a profitable sale from the first advertisement that cost little initially, creating a windfall of profits over time. This is the craft that you will be discovering and mastering, tweaking and improving as you go. A lot of money is wasted on paths that don't give business owners the return on investment they desire, and this is what you can fix when you apply ActionBrand Marketing.

Many random acts of marketing and advertising don't recover the investment. Or, they return just enough for the business owner to limp along, thinking they're accomplishing something.

What I'll share with you isn't the only way to the top of the mountain. But it's the most practical, sensible, efficient, and (I think you'll agree) wisest path to growing your business and putting cash in your pockets. We will go deeper into the how-to steps further into the book. The scope of this chapter is to give you a broad overview. In the previous chapters, we reviewed basic branding and marketing terms. We also discussed the eight big traps that lead to marketing and branding failure.

How ActionBrand Marketing Solves Your Business Growth Problems Once and for All

ActionBrand Marketing is a practical system that helps you achieve immediate cash flow, fast sales, and accelerated acceptance from branding over time. Let's start with two acronyms I have created to help you remember the main concepts: **ACTION** and **BRAND:**

ACTION stands for "Acquiring Clients Through Irresistible Offers Now."

A - Acquiring

C - Clients

T -Through

I – Irresistible

O - Offers

N- Now

I want you to internalize that because it is the essence of direct response marketing and advertising. Through direct response, we are no longer putting out vague advertisements saying:

"Call me!"

"Hire me now!"

"We're open!"

"We've been around since 1964!"

Instead, we offer specific solutions for specific problems aimed at specific audiences. When you switch traditional advertising to direct response advertising with specific offers, you will see a 200%, 300%, 400%, or more increase in ad response.

The second acronym I created is for the word **BRAND.**
**BRAND stands for "Broad Recognition of Affinity and Novel
Distinction."**

B - Broad

R - Recognition

A - Affinity

N - Novel

D - Distinction

Digest that for a minute. Broad Recognition of Affinity and
Novel Distinction. It means that branding intends to have your
specifically defined market recognize your company name and
anchor it to what you do uniquely and know that you do it specifically for THEM. This latter part is your company's affinity.
The Novel Distinction sets you apart from any other options and
makes you unique. We will go over how to do this in the correct
order. But at the end of the day, putting these two acronyms together produces a knockout combination.

Switch From Traditional Branding to ActionBrand Marketing

When I coach DJ entertainers and business owners, they often
mention needing to "work on their branding." What exactly does
that mean?

I find that most have a very naive notion of what "working on their branding and getting the word out" means in business. Their number one focus is often on what their logo should look like or what their company colors should be. They also tend to worry about what tag lines their company should use. These are secondary priorities since, as I mentioned earlier, they all mean nothing until the market knows you exist and why you are important to them. Any money spent on logos rather than spreading a clear message of the problems you solve and what you do to solve them only misses the target and winds up with little to no response.

If you run an ad and get no response, it may not be the media's fault. Can the media prove that it has a real readership with engaged viewers? If so, the problem is likely that your ad misses the mark in compelling that audience to pay attention, or the ad is missing a clear offer. It doesn't help if you complain to the media that sold you your ad campaign. They will tell you that you must keep running your ads for more exposure.

Why would you continue to run an ad that has gotten no response? It just doesn't make any sense! This is where you have to scrutinize your ad. If your ad received a little response, there might be hope and opportunity to improve it using methods you will learn in this book.

Low response happens when you run an ad with just your name, a fancy logo, and a meaningless tagline to a crowded market that doesn't know you. This is equivalent to just printing your business card. In the absence of any specific offer or value expressed, you will end up invisible. If your product or service is new or revolutionary, this problem is amplified.

This may seem counterintuitive. If you come up with something new, you may be jumping for joy because nobody has seen your product or service before. It might seem great at first. But your happiness can quickly turn to despair if your message falls on deaf ears because you use traditional branding. Simply put, most branding ads are concerned with look and image at the sacrifice of clarity and response.

Direct Response to Get Customers and Clients Fast

What I taught DJ business clients direct response marketing, their businesses changed forever. Legendary advertising expert David Ogilvy famously said:

"Only the mail-order guys know what they're doing. That's because the mail-order guys selling products on TV, radio, and in print ads were unconcerned about logos and 'look and feel.' They were offering exciting, interesting solutions to everyday problems and offering one and only one solution per advertisement, so you either took it or you didn't."

Here's a lesson: Even a big mail-order house with a vast catalog would be foolish if they tried to offer all their items in one advertisement. Instead, they offer their best-selling product in an advertisement because that one product brings in the most buyers. The buyers of that one low-price item become part of their list. Now, that mail-order house can send additional offers for related items or send their entire catalog to only those respondents, increasing response percentage because they are sending to "buyers," people who have voted for them by giving them money. Your dream list is a buyer list, which will save you tons of money in print and postage.

This direct response ad leads with a clear appeal and a clear offer for a response. Direct response can build your list and recover its investment quickly, leading to profit. If you sell one inexpensive "foot-in-the-door" offer, and the purchase not only pays for the item but the profit pays for the advertisement itself and gets one additional person on your mailing list to sell more items to, this would be a marketing utopia. You've created a self-liquidating advertisement, and you can effectively run that forever with an unlimited budget.

Where Does The Branding Come In?

In the ads I taught DJs to use, the logos were either at the bottom or not in the ad at all. It wasn't important until after they got a response. Any time you put that logo on, you are trading valuable content space, and it's a waste of real estate. It is essential to understand that branding takes a back seat to direct response at the early stage of your relationship with your market. But don't you fear! Branding begins to be added and sent to respondents for further communication, anchoring your name and "look and feel" with your audience.

ActionBrand Marketing to the Rescue

The central concept is to use direct response to gain attention in a new market, to achieve a response from that market in the form of sales, or at minimum, to collect their contact information for follow-up nurturing, and to grow your cash flow to snowball this process. Then branding is sent to the buyers, followers, and new fans to increase exponential reach.

You will begin sending branded messages and swag to your new audience because fans want something to be proud of. The idea behind ActionBrand Marketing is that those people only become raving fans once they've experienced you. But they don't choose to experience you because of a fancy name, logo, colors, or tagline. Instead, they choose you because they have a problem you have addressed with a desirable solution using strong direct response copy.

I'll reiterate. The purpose of direct response is to get buyers. The purpose of branding is to gain accelerated acceptance and exponential reach. This flywheel of business growth focuses on gathering happy clients and customers who stay, pay, and refer. These folks sing your praises, finally give your brand meaning, perhaps even wear your colors, and spread the word to others about what your brand means, bringing you new followers, repeat sales, and a platform to grow sales of your other products and services. This is when your brand matters and the cycle repeats.

KEY TAKEAWAYS

> - Introduce your value proposition to your target market first before focusing on branding.
> - Use direct response offers first to build your customer list.
> - Start branding once you've built an engaged prospect or buyers' list.
> - Your buyers' list becomes a branding platform to spread the word about your business' other products, services, and promotions. Get customers/clients and fans to build a brand.

In the coming chapters, let's unpack this and take it step-by-step.

Direct Response Marketing Orientation

"Nobody should be allowed to create general advertising until
he has served his apprenticeship in Direct-Response."

DAVID OGILVY, AKA THE FATHER OF ADVERTISING

Welcome to the world of Direct Response Marketing, where the ability to generate leads and drive sales is at your fingertips. This is the heart of ActionBrand Marketing.

Legendary business tycoon, David Ogilvy, known as "The Father of Advertising," spoke highly of Direct Response Marketing because of its ability to drive immediate response and accountability. Therefore, results for the advertiser, while advertising without direct response elements, were weaker and harder to measure.

In this chapter, I'll give you a crash course in Direct Response Marketing because it is the backbone and the "Action" part of ActionBrand Marketing. We will explore the strategies, techniques, and best practices that will empower you to leverage the full potential of Direct Response, the engine that powers ActionBrand Marketing.

A Brief History of Direct Response Advertising and Marketing

Although David Ogilvy is known as the father of advertising, Claude Hopkins is considered the father of direct response advertising. Ogilvy credits Hopkins with having changed his life through his introduction to his book "Scientific Advertising."

"Scientific Advertising" by Claude Hopkins, written in 1923, is a seminal work in the field of marketing, advocating the use of testing, measuring, and constant refinement in advertising. Hopkins argues for data-driven decisions over intuition, underscoring the importance of understanding customer psychology and behavior for effective advertising. Most, if not all, of the principles in the book, are as valid today as ever.

Regarding the book, Ogilvy stated, "Nobody, at any level, should be allowed to have anything to do with advertising until he has read this book seven times." Ogilvy added, "If you read this, you will never write another bad advertisement – and never approve one either."

The Difference Between Direct Response and Direct Marketing

People often use the terms "Direct Response" and "Direct Marketing" interchangeably, and it is a mistake because they ascribe to completely different methodologies. Direct Response refers to messages asking for a specific response in exchange for a particular offer. This could be simply asking for contact information in exchange for information or directly asking for the sale of a specific item, just like you see in mail order or TV infomercials.

Direct Marketing, on the other hand, merely describes selling directly to the public, rather than through a retailer, communicating through direct channels such as email, direct mail, or social media DMs, without using third-party or mass media. An example of this is Network Marketing. Said another way, Direct Response describes the mechanism of offer and response, while Direct Marketing is used to describe the channel or path from seller to buyer.

How Direct Response Marketing Compares to Awareness and Branding

These terms have substantial differences that, frankly, people have been unaware of, misunderstood, or have been misguided of. In this chapter, we will clear this up once and for all.

In advertising, there is a long-held principle that brands were established using PUBLICITY and then grown using AWARENESS THROUGH ADVERTISING. Brands focused their effort on getting in the news and then reminded people they existed via advertising.

As mentioned in previous chapters, building a brand through awareness can be a deep-pocket game because it relies on hard-to-control and unpredictable publicity, backed by paid advertising that seldom makes a clear offer to respond to.

Awareness campaigns show up and remind people of a brand's existence or repeat a tagline that seldom implies a response, like "Just Do It" (Nike) or "What Can Brown Do For You?" (UPS). Is that enough to get you to jump out of your seat to purchase?

DIRECT RESPONSE, on the other hand, will make an offer to solve a specific problem with a specific solution, inspiring action from the audience. Using a one problem, one solution approach simplifies the messaging, speaks to a specific audience in their own language, offers a solution to a specific problem that the audience desires, and ideally asks for an immediate response or purchase. The satisfied feeling of the <u>result</u> from that solution wins hearts and builds the brand!

The most clear illustration of Direct Response is mail order or the TV infomercial. One example was a little kitchen grill you likely know or own. Originally designed to cook fajitas, this invention initially garnered very little interest until the Salton company applied their Direct Response TV expertise to it, tweaked its application to burgers and other grill items, and attached an affable celebrity personality to it, giving the product the celebrity's namesake. The infomercial would offer the grill at a special price, with free shipping, and drove people to the phone lines, leading to over 100 million "George Foreman Grills" sold and still selling worldwide.

The Key Differences Between Direct Response Marketing and Traditional Marketing and Advertising Strategies

1. Measurability: One of the primary distinctions between Direct Response Marketing and traditional marketing lies in the ability to measure its effectiveness. Traditional marketing often relies on intangible metrics like brand awareness and sentiment, making quantifying the return on investment (ROI) challenging. Instead, Direct Response Marketing emphasizes measurable results, enabling businesses to track the success of their campaigns with precision. By analyzing metrics such as click-through rates, conversions, and sales, businesses can accurately evaluate their marketing efforts' impact.

2. Targeted Approach: Direct Response Marketing takes a laser-focused approach to reach the desired audience. Rather than casting a wide net and hoping to capture the attention of potential customers, it identifies specific segments and tailors messages to address their needs and desires directly. Businesses can create highly targeted campaigns that resonate with the intended recipients by understanding the target audience's demographics, interests, and pain points. This targeted approach enhances the likelihood of generating a response, leading to higher conversion rates.

3. Call-to-Action (CTA): Another critical distinction is the prominent role of a call-to-action in Direct Response Marketing. Traditional marketing often aims to build brand recognition and foster long-term relationships, which may not necessitate immediate action from the audience. In contrast, Direct Response Marketing relies on strong, persuasive CTAs that prompt the audience to take immediate action, such as purchasing, signing up for a newsletter, or requesting more information. These compelling CTAs create a sense of urgency and drive quick response, making Direct Response Marketing a powerful tool for lead generation and sales.

4. Personalization: Direct Response Marketing recognizes the importance of personalization in capturing the attention and interest of potential customers. Businesses can personalize their marketing messages by leveraging data and insights about the target audience to address specific pain points, desires, and preferences. This personal touch helps establish a connection with the audience, making them more likely to respond positively to the marketing campaign. Traditional marketing, on the other hand, often relies on generic messaging that may resonate less strongly with individual recipients.

5. Testing and Optimization: Direct Response Marketing heavily emphasizes testing and optimization. By continually testing different elements of their campaigns, such as headlines, offers, and visuals, businesses can identify the most effective strategies and refine their approach over time. This iterative process allows for continuous improvement and maximizes the ROI of marketing efforts. In contrast, traditional marketing strategies may not prioritize testing and optimization to the same extent, potentially missing out on opportunities for growth and refinement.

Direct Response Marketing differs from traditional marketing in its measurability, targeted approach, emphasis on strong CTAs, personalization, and focus on testing and optimization. By understanding these key differences, businesses can harness the power of Direct Response within the ActionBrand Marketing framework to generate leads, drive sales, and achieve remarkable growth.

The Fundamentals of ActionBrand Marketing Direct Response

I was introduced to Hopkin's work by Dan Kennedy, who further taught me the power of Direct Response Marketing. In essence, he taught me that the principles used in mail order advertising to drive immediate, measurable sales can be used to promote any business more effectively than traditional advertising alone.

Over the years, I have developed my proprietary formula for Direct Response Marketing blended with Branding, which I call ActionBrand Marketing.

The acronym I invented to teach my methodology is the "A.C.T. N.O.W." formula.

A.C.T. N.O.W. FORMULA

- **AUDIENCE(S)**
- **CHANNEL(S)**
- **TRANSACTION**

- **NURTURE**
- **OFFERS**
- **WOW YOUR BUYERS**

AUDIENCE

Not everyone will resonate with your message or product in the vast ocean of consumers. That's where the principle of the Target Audience comes into play. Understanding your target audience isn't merely about recognizing a broad demographic; it's about delving into the psychographics, the very essence of the customer's wants, needs, and pain points.

The Customer Avatar: Your Ideal Customer

Imagine your perfect client or customer. Who are they? What do they like? What are their fears, dreams, and aspirations? This conceptualization is known as a "Customer Avatar". By crafting a precise, detailed avatar, you visually represent the person most likely to buy your product or service.

Your target audience is a grouping of folks that exhibit the psychographics of this customer avatar. Your marketing message must be tailored to resonate with this group, essentially acting as a magnet that attracts only those perfectly aligned with what you offer.

Here is an illustrative example: Let's say you're marketing a boutique fitness studio. Your customer avatar could be a 39-year-old recently divorced woman who loves ladies' nights, reads specific magazines, worries about her overall health and appearance, and is willing to invest in premium coaching.

Your customer avatar should be as vivid as a character in a movie, encompassing not just age, gender, and location, but hobbies, interests, pain points, objections, and even favorite media channels. I've learned of companies that go as far as to give their avatar a name, like "Ashley." Every time the company would have a meeting when making decisions, they would ask the group, "What would Ashley think of this?" On a side note, if you want to copy this exercise and give your avatar a name, Google the most popular names given to folks born in the years that your avatar (male or female) would have been born and choose from the list. This multidimensional understanding will guide every aspect of your marketing, from copywriting to channel selection, which we will discuss next.

CHANNEL

Choosing the channel involves selecting and utilizing the most appropriate and effective media channels to reach your target audience. Whether television, radio, social media, email, or direct mail, your chosen channel must align with where your customer avatar spends their time and seeks information.

Think of your customer avatar once again. Social media platforms might be your primary channel if they're a tech-savvy millennial. If they're a busy executive, industry-specific magazines or targeted email or direct mail campaigns may be a consideration.

TRANSACTION

Once you've successfully identified your customer avatar and found the proper channels to reach them, your work is far from over. Your next step is to decide what outcome you want from each communication, which I call "transactions."

Depending on the type of service or product you have to offer, do you want the audience to buy something, or do you want to collect contact information to build a list?

These decisions are very situational, and there are many ways to be right. For the purpose of this crash course, I will recommend the most important transaction first, which is the lead generation transaction.

The Lead Generation Transaction

Suppose you sell a high-ticket product or service requiring a more in-depth explanation or personalized analysis before someone could invest. Then, you would craft an offer that would entice the prospect to exchange their contact information for something of value you would provide. This thing of value is referred to as a "lead magnet." It could be some valuable information, a video, an offer of free consultation, or even a physical product you give away for free.

The First Sale Transaction

Sometimes, you may choose to sell a small-ticket, entry product, or service as a first sale transaction. Again, this is very situational, and you should perform testing to see if this is the smart approach for your particular situation.

The pro to a small-ticket first transaction is that it acts as a filter because you know that a paying buyer is more likely to buy your high-ticket offers than a freebie seeker. The trade-off would be that you will end up with a much smaller list to nurture; however, the list you get will be of greater value. Many marketers argue that they would rather have a smaller list of buyers than a massive list of "suspects."

In a mature business, you would have a family of transactions, some free and some entry-level, all functioning simultaneously. There are many ways to be correct and many moving parts and testing over time that must occur to determine your path.

Your job is to test your objectives constantly. As you find a winner, call it the "control." As you test other campaigns, always consider "beating the control."

If you are lucky, you may discover an offer that works for years. In too many cases, offers go lame over time due to fatigue (seeing the offer so much it becomes invisible or ignored) or change in culture or human behaviors and beliefs (a sign of the times).

That is why the job of the professional is never done, as we are always testing.

NURTURE

Nurturing these prospects is the next crucial step in your Direct Response Marketing journey. In this context, nurturing means developing and strengthening relationships with potential customers at every stage of the sales funnel.

Understanding that most prospects will not convert into customers immediately is essential. They may be interested or intrigued by your product or service but not ready to purchase. The late Chet Holmes stated that as little as 3% of any market is ready to buy, and that is where most small businesses focus their efforts, leaving lots of opportunity on the table. This stage is where nurturing comes in. It's like tending a field of crops; with the right amount of care and attention, you can yield a profitable harvest.

Prospects who have shown interest in your offering but have yet to buy are considered "warm leads." Nurturing these leads could involve a series of emails, informative content, personalized offers, or regular check-ins. The goal is to build trust and get people to like you by keeping consistent touch with valuable content and keeping your brand at the top of their minds when they are ready to purchase.

OFFERS

When you have built an audience and a list of people who would be responsive to your messages and have been giving value through informative emails, videos, and other propaganda (I mean this lovingly), it's time to monetize by making offers.

An offer is more than just the product or service you're selling; it's a package that includes the price, terms, bonuses, guarantees, and, most importantly, the unique value proposition. The best offers are customer-centric, solving a problem or fulfilling a desire of your customer avatar. They are not merely transactions but exchanges of value.

While your initial "transaction" may have involved a free offer to collect contact information to build your list, it is time to harvest its value now that your list has been warmed.

The Irresistible Offer

Start with your intuition and ask yourself, "What would my avatar's most pressing problem be, and what solution can I offer them that is so valuable they cannot say no?" We call this an "irresistible offer."

An irresistible offer is a blend of high perceived value and a sense of urgency. The value could come from the core product, bonuses, discounts, or exclusive features. Meanwhile, the urgency could be created by limited quantities, a countdown timer, or a special occasion linked to discounts or bonuses.

To create an irresistible offer, you must understand your customer avatar deeply, knowing what they perceive as valuable and what would motivate them to act quickly.

The Offer Ladder or Wheel of Offers

You want to craft a "family" of offers, and your job is to test what order they should be presented constantly. Look at it like a "ladder" or "wheel" of offers.

If your service or products work well together, you can determine an order of importance in which you believe your customer or client will want to invest. Then, you can periodically walk them through other steps of your ladder or rungs in your wheel.

Here is a real-world example: Invicta watches offers a low-price wristwatch, and part of their irresistible offer includes an eight or 25-slot watch case valued at $79.00 for free. Why would they include a 25-slot watch case with the purchase of one watch? They are imposing the human impulse of collecting, similar to stamp collecting or other collectibles. Many folks simply cannot stand not filling those empty slots. Brilliant!

Your bottom line will be directly linked to your offers' success and optimized pricing, the optimized cadence, how often you make them to your audience and list, and any continuity or recurring subscriptions in your wheelhouse.

Making a Promise of Transformation

Every great offer promises a transformation. This transformation might be big, like a career change program promising a new life, or smaller, like a skincare product promising a clearer complexion. Your offer should paint a vivid picture of this "after state," making the benefits clear and tangible.

Always Be Testing

Finally, the effectiveness of your offer should be continuously tested and refined. Use A/B testing to see which elements resonate most with your audience. Small changes, like a different bonus or a stronger call to action, can sometimes significantly impact conversion rates.

In Direct Response Marketing, your offer(s) is(are) the moment of truth. It's where your understanding of your customer avatar, channel marketing, and nurturing efforts come together. By crafting an irresistible offer, you're not just selling a product or service but offering a path to a desired outcome. And when this offer aligns perfectly with your audience's needs and desires, the results can be extraordinary.

WOW YOUR BUYERS FOR ENDLESS RETURNS

Congratulations! Your audience selection, choice of media channel, lead generation, diligent nurturing, and impeccable offer crafting have translated into a sale. Your relationship is only beginning because you don't just want a one-time purchase; you want a love affair! The real success of Direct Response Marketing is measured not only by the first transaction but by the ability to cultivate loyal customers who come back time and again and tell others about you.

I. Deliver More Than Expected

The first step to wowing your buyer is to overdeliver. This could include an unexpected bonus product, expediting shipping at no extra cost, or simply offering a handwritten thank-you note with their purchase. Little unexpected gestures can create a lasting positive impression.

2. Stellar Customer Service

Never underestimate the power of genuine, responsive customer service. Address concerns promptly, handle returns or complaints gracefully, and always maintain a courteous tone. A positive customer service experience can turn a disgruntled customer into a loyal, raving fan.

3. Engage Post-Purchase

Engage your buyers even after the sale. Offer them valuable content, insights, or exclusive previews of upcoming products. Consider implementing a loyalty program or a referral discount. Keep the lines of communication open, and show genuine interest in their feedback and experience with your product or service.

4. Continuous Value Addition

Consistently introduce new products or updates that align with your buyers' evolving needs and desires. When you continually add value to their lives, they'll have a reason to return.

5. Personalization Goes a Long Way

With the advances in data analytics, tailor the shopping experience for repeat buyers. Recommend products based on their purchase history, or offer personalized discounts. Recognize milestones in your relationship, like the anniversary of their first purchase, with special offers or messages.

6. Survey your Fans and Give Them What They Want

Feedback is a goldmine. It offers insights directly from your customers, telling you what you're doing right and where you can improve. But collecting feedback isn't enough; acting on it is where you show your customers that their opinions matter.

When you wow your buyers, you do more than ensure a repeat purchase. You turn them into brand ambassadors, individuals who'll sing your praises to others. In Direct Response Marketing, where the focus is so profoundly centered on the customer, the adage is true: treat your customers right, and they'll do the marketing for you. You are getting PAID to build your brand. THIS is how you build a brand the ActionBrand Marketing way!

KEY TAKEAWAYS

- Direct Response Marketing drives immediate responses and accountability.
- Direct Response delivers solutions, provoking instant action.
- A.C.T. N.O.W. formula: Audience, Channel, Transaction, Nurture, Offers, and Wow Your Buyers.
- Customer Avatars allow you to target messages effectively.
- Choose channels aligned with Customer Avatar habits.
- Craft offers that promise transformation, are irresistible, and create a ladder of value.
- Nurturing builds relationships through engagement and trust.
- Wowing buyers fosters loyalty and advocacy.

The DNA of an ActionBrand

"Branding and Marketing are the deliberate crafting
of perception for the winning of Heart Share."

MARK IMPERIAL

Why are we toiling over ActionBrand Marketing? Because nothing else matters unless someone buys something. And no one buys things until they hear about them. And no one hears about anything unless something grabs their attention. And when that attention turns them into raving fans, you gain ambassadors who can make sure more and more people hear about you.

ActionBrand Marketing is the craft of grabbing attention, inspiring action, making an indelible impression in the mind, and ultimately gaining raving fans.

In business, we talk about gaining "market share" in a category. Advanced thinkers create "categories of one" where they can own market dominance.

In ActionBrand Marketing, I call it "Winning Heart Share." I believe that expression is a more useful way to view the goal because it constantly reminds us of the emotional connection we always want to craft.

WINNING "HEART SHARE" WITH ACTIONBRAND MARKETING

Branding wins hearts when it resonates with audiences at an emotional, intellectual, and sometimes even spiritual level. The power of branding lies in its ability to communicate the essence of a product, service, or company and align it with the values, aspirations, and desires of its target audience.

The Direct Response style of Marketing, which is at the heart of ActionBrand Marketing, is also called "Emotional Direct Response" because we aim to connect with our audience emotionally. Great ActionBrand Marketing tells a story. It taps into emotions, experiences, and perhaps even memories. Brands like Apple, Harley-Davidson, and Rolex don't just sell products; they sell aspirations, dreams, and a sense of belonging.

Here are several other ways that ActionBrand Marketing wins hearts:

- **Authenticity:** People resonate with genuine, honest, and transparent brands.

- **Consistency:** Brands that maintain a consistent image, message, and quality across all touchpoints (like advertisements, packaging, and user experience) build trust with their audience. Delivering or over-delivering on your brand promises also fosters loyalty.

- **Shared Values:** People will bond deeply with those brands that promote values that are important to them. Lego, for example, has won many hearts by promoting the value of "creativity" and empowering children and adults alike to imagine and create without boundaries.

- **Engagement:** Engagement-driven brand building is about building trust, establishing two-way communication, and often co-creating value with the audience. GoPro positioned itself as a lifestyle brand rather than just a company selling cameras. They engage their audience by encouraging them to share their action-packed videos, and they often showcase user-generated content in their marketing campaigns.

- **Sensory Appeal:** There are many things to consider that appeal to the senses, from the appearance to the tactile feel to the ambiance, mood, or feeling that your product or service exudes. Smell, taste, or sound also make impressions. Tiffany & Co. made their iconic "Tiffany Blue" box evoke strong emotions before even seeing the jewelry inside. The distinct roar of a Ferrari engine has become synonymous with the brand.

- **Community Building:** An early mentor of mine once said that "people are walking around with their umbilical cord in their hand looking for a place to plug it in." Harley-Davidson has a passionate community of riders. The Harley Owners Group (HOG) is a well-known club that organizes rides and events that are a huge part of the brand's identity. Starbucks touted itself as the "third place" between work and home, giving a sense of community and belonging.

- **Innovation:** Your raving fans get excited by "what's next," and you can gain audiences with each exciting new announcement. You can lose a community if you don't appear ahead of the curve. Keep thinking of your "what's next." Amazon and Netflix started as purveyors of physical products, but both have evolved into juggernauts of digital media, cloud computing, and streaming. Both brands are now playing with the big dogs as movie studios.

- **Social Responsibility/Positive Impact:** People connect with positive movements. Related to shared values, these causes can tip a sale. TOMS shoes built its brand on the promise that they would donate a pair to a child in need for every pair of shoes purchased. This "One for One" concept allowed the purchasers to feel like a participant in the contribution.

I've read many books on branding and marketing over the last 25 years, and each gives a version of a method to memorialize your uniqueness. The term "elevator pitch" has a foggy history, but in essence, it is an intentionally crafted and memorized message containing your concepts and ideas which is short enough to be delivered and understood during a brief period of time, like a conversation during a 30-second elevator ride.

The elevator pitch's uniqueness component conveys your business' USP or unique selling proposition. TV advertising pioneer Rosser Reeves coined USP in the 1940s. Your unique selling proposition identifies something that you or your company does differently or uniquely versus any other competitors in your category so you can stand out.

My mentor, Dan Kennedy, further popularized the concept with his famous question that helps you uncover your uniqueness. The question is, "Why should I (Mr. Prospect) do business with you over any other option available to me, including doing nothing at all?" Dan's question is a terrific starting point to discover any business' USP or uniqueness.

HOW A ONE-WORD DNA APPEAL TURNED A FAILING COMPANY INTO THE FASTEST-GROWING MULTI-BILLION DOLLAR BRAND

In 1995, I attended the first "Battle of the Masters" martial arts show in Chicago. It was an eight-man, winner-take-all, no holds barred (with the exception of eye gouging and biting) tournament. I started karate lessons in 1982, and questions around the dojo were always about which martial arts would win against another. So this was a utopia for karate practitioners. Keep in mind this is a very niche thing because only some are karate practitioners.

The Battle of the Masters did not come first. It was inspired by the first mixed martial arts organization known today as the Ultimate Fighting Championships. It began in 1993 with a tiny fan base consisting mainly of karate enthusiasts like myself. I was so excited when I saw the promotion for the first UFC pay-per-view in November 1993. I purchased it immediately, so my closest friends gathered around the TV as I taped it on a VHS tape. I still have that tape today! It's funny because since I taped it live, it includes all of the horrible amateur commentary that has since been edited out of the available video today.

Anyway, the tiny fan base of martial arts enthusiasts gathered around their televisions with nervous excitement and anticipation as fights were about to take place between different disciplines from Karate, Judo, Taekwondo, boxing, and even sumo wrestling! Which style was going to come out on top? We were finally going to find out, at least we thought! The outcome was shocking because the winning style was Brazilian jiu-jitsu, which most of the world had never heard of before!

Moving forward, that led to follow-up events like UFC 2, 3, 4, and so on. However, the idea never really took off but rather went downhill. If you didn't know the history, you would hardly believe it, considering what the UFC looks like today.

The downfall came from relentless backlash from the public and politicians. Politicians led many states to ban UFC events. In 1997, the shows were forced "underground," practically making them invisible. The company was bleeding money.

By 2000, UFC's parent company SEG was teetering on the brink of bankruptcy. The exhausted SEG happily sold the company when approached with a measly 2 million dollar offer.

The new owners did one thing to save the company and turn it into the fastest-growing sport and a multi-billion dollar brand that sold for over 4 billion dollars and is still growing.

So what happened?

HOW A ONE-WORD CHANGE IN DNA CREATED A FORTUNE

The new owners deliberately did one thing that saved the company and got the public to catch fire behind the brand.

It wasn't an overnight success. By 2004, the new owners had racked up 34 million dollars in losses since buying the company. They had one final idea that they would double down on.

In 2005, they approached Spike TV with an idea for a reality TV show that they were willing to fund themselves with production costs of 10 million dollars. If they were going out, they would go out on their sword.

Well, it was an instant (12-year) success. Viewers came in droves, and the "UFC" was the hottest "new" thing the public was hearing about and loving.

What was the difference?

The DNA

Remember the DNA is the basic feeling and personality of the brand. It is what is in the mind of the consumer. It is their preconceived notions of who you are and what you are about.

The first tagline for UFC was "There are no rules." They promoted the brutality. They bet on shock value. Teeth flying. Nut kicks. I watched a guy give non-stop groin punches. Dumb shit, really. That goes to show you that car-crash-type appeal can only get you so far.

How Did They Change the DNA?

The new reality show focused on the fighters as real people. Like the boxing build-up shows, it reflected their hopes, dreams, and family life. Most importantly, they showed disciplined training behind the scenes; until now, nobody really saw.

The show reflected the new RULES that were in place. It was no longer "no rules"; there was standardization. There were weight classes—no more 600 lb Sumo vs. 145 lb Muay Thai fighter. The fighters evolved to now learn the most effective techniques from other disciplines. Martial Arts took its most significant step forward in evolution. Although purists like myself would credit Bruce Lee for creating Mixed Martial Arts with my favorite quote, "Absorb what is useful. Reject what is useless. Add what is essentially your own," UFC gets credit for bringing it to the masses.

The DNA, the sentiment in the public's mind, shifted from "SPECTACLE" to "SPORT." No longer seen as human cock-fighting, UFC gained tremendous traction and a gigantic fan base in a short time. Note that UFC is the brand, but the sport they put on the map is "MMA" or "Mixed Martial Arts." If you say MMA to someone, there's a big chance they'll respond, "Oh,

UFC." As a hobby, I used to coach at Ricardo Lamas' UFC Gym in Naperville, Illinois, and we joked that people who train in MMA say, "We do UFC."

This is an example of how critical the DNA of your company is. How do you want the world to think about your business? Who or what do you stand for? Who or what do you stand against? Answer this question with every piece of content and ensure the world anchors these sentiments in the mind.

DNA AND UNIQUE SELLING PROPOSITION

Some examples of uniqueness can come from guarantees, speed of delivery, or speed of results. The famous Domino's Pizza's unique selling point was, "Hot, fresh pizza delivered in 30 minutes or less guaranteed!" This message built an empire.

The way you come to your USP is to look at what everyone else in your industry is saying about themselves, cross out everything common among them, and find a gap, something they're not talking about. This missing piece must be something you know is valuable to your prospects.

Distinction of Novel Appeal

In ActionBrand Marketing, I refer to this as "DNA," which stands for Distinction of Novel Appeal. I believe that DNA is more appropriate because it can be spread among sibling products and services to be known as a "family." The idea is to find a unique, appealing point for your prospect. My method's idea is to make it more conversational and natural rather than robotic and contrived.

If you want a complete, up-to-date list of inspirations for your DNA statement, go to **actionbrandmarketing.com** and download the book resources, where you will find the checklist for DNA statements.

There are many formulas for USPs, yet few discuss their applications. The formulas tend to create sentences that sound a bit weird when spoken conversationally. For example, a typical USP using an old formula can sound like, "Books written for you that sound like you wrote them without you writing a single word in less than 30 days, guaranteed!" Do you see how this might be clear but sounds robotic and contrived?

Now, a USP like that can serve as an internal guiding statement so that you stay on track with your business and how you build it together with your deliverables, but it needs cleaning up if you want to use it conversationally and attract clients. For example, changing that USP into a DNA statement can sound like this: "You know how many executives want to be published authors but don't have the time to write or think writing is too much work? Our professional writing team turns executives' knowledge into a book in about a month that is so good, their own mothers would believe they wrote it."

The ultimate test of your DNA statement is if your listener asks to hear more. An example is if they ask you, "How do you do that?" In other words, did you create fascination? Did you elicit a conversation? Or did they smile and look confused? Of course, it also matters if your listener is someone who would be interested in your solution in the first place.

Start With "Who Is Your Ideal Customer or Client?"

Before you come up with your Distinction of Novel Appeal, you must determine what audience you want attention from. Refer to the chapter on direct response marketing for the topic of audience and customer avatar.

Pillow Talk

Once you have identified your ideal audience, that audience has common problems. Your products or services should address those common problems directly. Ask yourself, "What big issues keep these folks awake at night? What worries them so much that they lie awake at night, head on the pillow, sharing their worries with their spouse?" This is what we call "pillow talk." Author Robert Collier famously said, "Always enter the conversation already taking place in the customer's mind."

Talk about your audience and their problems, not about you. Present your solution or offer after you have gotten their attention by demonstrating you know their pain. Remember, if you can describe someone's pain better than they can, or when nobody else addresses it, you can grab their attention.

DNA and Naming Your Company and Products/Services

Here you will discover a clarifying way to explain your business and products starting with your company name and the names of your products and services. Because the branding takes place simultaneously to direct marketing sales, we need these clarifications in place.

First, let's start with understanding a few terms: your company, your products/services, and how to brand each. First and foremost, as a reminder, the goal of the branding element of action branding is to create a BRAND that stands for Broad Recognition of Affinity and Novel Distinction in your target audience's mind.

You must anchor your brand's name with your novel distinction and meanings to create a BRAND. You must maintain those meanings. Accordingly, you need to choose brand names carefully.

If you already have a company name, consider this question: Does your name clearly communicate what you do and how your company's products or services help your prospects? If it does, great. If not, then you may want to consider a few things.

Consider changing your name if your company name is not yet anchored to the public and they don't know you or identify with your name. If it's anchored already, think about sub-branding by considering certain factors.

There's a lot of talk in the branding community about creating an almost nonsensical or unrelated word to brand something. That's why we have names like Amazon, Nike, and Pixar. According to the book "22 Immutable Laws of Branding", these names are good because they don't break the law of the generic name, i.e., "Shoes.com" or "Books.com." I will point out, however, that those companies had the luxury of practically unlimited budgets and spent hundreds of millions of dollars to anchor their names in the consumers' minds. This method should not be considered first if you don't have the desire or ability to wait 50 years for traction and an endless pot of money to get you there at your disposal.

Let's talk about parent companies first. Procter & Gamble is an example of a parent company or what they refer to as the master brand or mega brand. The name Procter & Gamble often means something only to people within the industry, but P&G's brands are what the public knows. Brands such as Crest, Gillette, Pampers, and Tide don't use P&G's name in the spotlight. Instead, each of these products is branded separately because they have individual meanings in different categories.

In some cases, the company is used as the brand name for the product. For example, the Coca-Cola Company owns Coca-Cola and Coke. By the way, the nickname "Coke" came from consumers to shorten the product's name when talking about it, and in 1945, the company made it official and trademarked the word "Coke." Coca-Cola and Coke are used as references because they've been anchored as the same product in consumers' minds.

To simplify these factors, consider this: Your company name can have one overriding DNA or Distinction of Novel Appeal. What is the novel appeal of your company? What distinguishes your work from your comparables?

I say comparables and not competition because, ideally, we want to create a perception of no competition since you do things differently. This has been called a blue ocean strategy, popularized by a book of the same name.

Take the case of my own company. My company's name is Imperial Action, and it has an overriding DNA that states, "Helping business owners and professionals communicate their message to the world so their businesses grow."

Currently, my company has two focuses. First, my sub-brand, Books Grow Business, helps professionals and business owners memorialize their methods in a book that they use to attract clients and close deals faster. The DNA of my sub-brand, Books Grow Business, is "Helping professionals and business owners clearly establish their identities and memorialize their methods in a signature book so clients easily choose them."

Second, my agency brand is Imperial Action, which I consider the master or mega brand. My agency brand's DNA is "Helping business owners and professionals show up top of mind through consistent communication so they can acquire clients and customers consistently and predictably."

Notice that my Imperial Action brand's DNA is about clarifying and communicating a message to the world. My Books Grow Business brand is about creating a signature book. Imperial Action is a multi-media agency that helps professionals create consistent weekly content and distribute it to multiple platforms and media such as video, audio, print, and text. In my case, Imperial Action is the master or mega brand, so I'm using it like Coca-Cola or WD-40 because WD-40 is a lubricant made by the WD-40 Company, and the Coca-Cola company makes Coca-Cola.

The core message of my master brand is in line with that particular service, so I chose to use it rather than come up with a different name. This allows my direct response marketing to have more impact with the name Imperial Action.

Having these clear distinctions in place simplifies your communications and gives you a filter to use whenever you create new marketing content or offers. Before putting out a message, ask yourself if the message clearly bolsters the position you have or want to have in the minds of your prospects. It's important to have this in place before anything else.

The task of crafting company names and brand names is both simple and complicated at the same time. Because no one size fits all, and each company has different paths, seek consultation with a professional in ActionBranding for advice on your specific circumstance. To find a certified ActionBrand Marketing Guide, visit: www.actionbrandmarketing.com.

KEY TAKEAWAYS

> Elevator pitches are concise messages conveying ideas in a short span.

> Unique Selling Proposition (USP) highlights your business's uniqueness.

> USP discovery involves answering why you over other options.

> UFC's transformation highlights the power of shifting DNA, as changing DNA from spectacle to sport altered public perception.

> DNA shapes your brand's personality in consumers' minds.

> Distinction of Novel Appeal (DNA) finds unique, conversational points.

> Effective DNA statements prompt curiosity and conversations.

> Addressing customer problems is key to crafting a compelling DNA.

> Strategic naming anchors meanings and simplifies communication.

The Five Branding Trust Triggers (Five Marketing Love Languages)

> "People will do anything for those who encourage their dreams, justify their failures, allay their fears, confirm their suspicions, and help them throw rocks at their enemies."
>
> BLAIR WARREN

As you craft the DNA of your brand, there is a straightforward concept with five parts that can help guide you to make your ongoing messaging consistent. I call this "The Five Branding Trust Triggers" or "The Five Marketing Love Languages."

Since ActionBranding starts with direct response, you will communicate different messages and offers to the world. These five trust triggers will help you craft messages that will telegraph your company's personality deliberately and consistently.

What Are Trust Triggers?

Trust triggers are shortcuts and identifiers that build trust with prospective listeners or readers. You can do this through teaching, demonstrations, stories, and educational case studies from real clients. The idea behind trust triggers is that you subtly implant your company's personality in your audience's mind with every message you put out. The objective is to capture the essence of your company and own a place in your audience's mind.

Trust triggers create sentiments that elicit trust. You can see dramatic increases in engagement and response when you address specific sentiments in your marketing message. The beauty of this system is that there are only five sentiments to focus on, so there are fewer things to think about. In fact, addressing anything beyond these five trust triggers can be perceived as unnecessary noise. The good news is this system simplifies your marketing.

To explain the power of trust triggers clearly, I will share examples I give my media coaching students when they prepare for radio. These are clients I help prepare for guest appearances on radio talk shows. I teach them how to speak about their business in the context of the five trust triggers. Their answers to the radio host's questions can become daily, weekly, or monthly marketing content.

Since they are speaking on the radio, I train them to talk in soundbites. Speaking in soundbites is an excellent exercise in clarifying your message and communicating it in the most compact and accessible form for others to receive and understand.

As I share these examples, pretend that a radio show host is asking you the same questions about your business. Consider how you would answer these questions.

Trust Trigger #1: Affinity

Even if your product or service solves a wide range of problems for many people, people want to feel as if it was made just for them. This is why you will see the same product packaged differently to serve different audiences. Remember that with the affinity trigger, prospects want to know if you understand their problem. It starts by speaking in the language of the prospect, not in the language of your industry or peers.

Napoleon Hill told the story of Andrew Carnegie's mother going into a store to buy a little furnace. Rather than probing the lady about what she truly desired and listening intently, the salesperson began lecturing her on BTUs, energy efficiency, and quality. The little old lady interrupted the salesperson to ask, *"Son, will this keep a little old lady warm?"* Be aware that you must speak in layperson's terms rather than in your industry's language.

Here's an example: If the radio host asks you, "Tell me a little about your business, and specifically, tell us who are the types of clients and customers you serve?" Your answer could be, "Thanks, Mark. We help so and so with so and so." And then, you share why they want to achieve this outcome. Let's say your business is physical therapy or chiropractic. Your answer to the host's question could be, "ABC Wellness specializes in helping athletes achieve full mobility and maximum recovery quickly, so they gain an edge over their competition." This particular answer hones in on athletes, although your company may treat regular people, stay-at-home moms, and corporate executives. Think of your audience and who you want to attract.

Trust Trigger #2: The Provider

This trust trigger involves sharing the stories or case studies of similar clients. You want to plant seeds of experience with your prospect because the provider has to be seen as someone who understands and knows a specific problem very well. People want to see themselves in your examples and think, "That's me!" The prospects want to know if you are qualified to solve their problem. Folks want to know your views about what they perceive are their problems because they're not just buying the product or the service; they're also buying you as the provider. Even if the service may be a commodity, the number one thing in your prospects' minds is, as the provider, "Can I trust *you*?"

Interestingly, people with higher incomes hire you more for who you are than for what you do because what you do may be a commodity. People will pay more for a perceived bona fide expert. That is why people are eager to author books on particular topics - they want to be seen as leaders in their field. Authorship instantly gives them a pay raise that is readily accepted. You want to be seen as the obvious expert who knows a subject inside and out.

That's why I love interviews, and spotlight interview content is a superb form of marketing. Your audience is accustomed to interviews, having listened to talk radio or watching talk shows on TV like Oprah, so it is an easy-to-digest format, which is a huge benefit. When you present your marketing content in an interview format, you're seen as the obvious expert. Interview content is about demonstrating your expertise, being spotlighted on the radio, and being interviewed and asked intelligent questions allowing you to shine. Because you are answering the host, you're talking in a third-person conversation, yet you are demonstrating you know your subject cold without sounding like you're bragging.

Can you see the subtlety in interview marketing? You're not talking to your prospects directly and saying, "Well, I'm the number one in this because I achieved this, and look at the awards I've got." The interview does that for you. The interviewer host anoints you as the expert. You must humbly insert information about your origin story in this trust trigger. This is where you can talk about how you became an expert at solving a particular problem and discovered the solutions. You can also talk about overcoming obstacles and how you got your start.

If a radio host asks you what inspired you to get into your field, it's your opportunity to talk about a specific time or an event when you caught the bug to do what it is that you do. You can talk about what drives you, your passion, your work, and how you help people. The interview is about what you say and how you say it. The late Zig Ziglar said, "Sales is nothing but a transference of feeling."

When you're passionate, people can feel it. When you know something works and believe in it, it will show because it worked for you, and you've helped others with it. The passion oozes out of you. You should create your origin story and get in the habit of constantly fine-tuning it over time. Keep in mind that, besides money, people want to know that there is another honorable motivation for your work. You should highlight this motivation somewhere in your story.

Can you find a way to link what you're doing today with any stories from your childhood? I'll give an example of how I did that for my DJ entertainment business. When promoting and marketing my DJ entertainment services to corporations, I would share stories demonstrating that I was "born to be an entertainer." I could go back to my childhood and think of some adventures, like, my dad foolishly but lovingly taking me to a KISS concert in 1976. I was a goofy seven or eight-year-old kid at that time and the only kid in that marijuana-filled auditorium, but I digress.

I then go on to tell the rest of the story. When I returned from that concert, for the next two weeks, I and my posse of kid friends would put on my mom's make-up, make KISS costumes out of our pajamas, and put on fake KISS concerts in our living room. And I've got pictures to prove it. For me, entertaining and being in the spotlight started at a young age. I was fortunate enough to have kept those pictures to use in my marketing.

I had many other stories. I had gone on to breakdancing and started teaching it at the local library. When the moonwalk was brand new, and nobody had seen Michael Jackson do that yet, I did the moonwalk in a variety show in my high school as a last-minute fill-in. It was just a goof, but I got six standing ovations. All of these moments are parts of my origin story. When people hear these, they would conclude that it's no wonder I'm an entertainer and started a DJ company. So the implication is that I love what I do so much, have been doing it so long that I must be good, and money wasn't the prime motivator.

Your background story should show how you caught the bug to do what you're doing now. It should also demonstrate that you are driven and passionate about what you do and for the people you do it for. It is not only a money thing for you. Please answer what inspired you to do what you do and internalize it whenever you are asked.

Trust Trigger #3: The Method

Use this trigger to tactfully show the value exchange of what you do against other options available to your audience, including doing nothing at all. People always think, "My business is different. Is your solution going to work for me?" This is your opportunity to address your particular prospect's number one problem. Let me give you a sample question from a radio host.

Using the physical therapy example in the previous case study, a radio host might ask, "What is the most common problem your athletes face in achieving mobility?" Think about the version of this question in your field. Another question for the physical therapy example could be, "How can athletes successfully overcome this problem to achieve full mobility?" And here's where you can describe how you've helped an athlete, specifically in overcoming the problem you identified. That way, you communicate to a specific audience.

Here's one possible answer to the question: "Great question, Mark. I had a client who had an accident. In that accident, this is what occurred, and this is how we helped him". My answer shows the audience that I understood the athlete's problem and had helped people just like them with the exact problem. I showed them an example of my methods and told the story, from diagnosing the problem to applying solutions to the final outcome. This gives prospects a clear picture of whether my solution will work for them.

You can include information about how the athletes overcame obstacles and what they could have done to avoid them, or you can share an unpleasant consequence that you helped them avoid. You can also bring up some of the biggest things on your prospects' minds that keep them from taking action and sabotage their success. You can bring this up to give them a good reason to act. For example, is it time commitment that causes people to procrastinate? Is it the price of the solution or service? Did they think it would not work? You can show how your solution worked to fulfill past customers' needs.

Here's an example answer for that particular question: "You know how most business owners think that the market is the problem? Well, they find out in reality that the market is usually not the problem, but the marketing or lack of it."

Then you can explain by saying, "I'll give you an example. I had a client that (fill in the blank). But the reality is they were not doing anything to reach that market, or they used the wrong media for their marketing". Do you see where I'm going with this? I'm giving an example that lets my prospects know I understand their problem and have a crystal ball to show them the way.

Trust Trigger #4: The Value Proposition

Prospects want to know, "Is this a good value? What will I get from this, and at what cost? What do I risk? What are the risks of using a different solution besides this one? Will I potentially waste more money using a different solution, or will I lose money by doing nothing to solve this problem?" These are some of the questions you can address with this trust trigger of value.

If your call to action is to get a free consultation, they may want to know if it's valuable enough to invest their time in having a phone call with you. How difficult do you make it to get information? This is where you want to make an offer to provide more information that is valuable and risk-free. For example, perhaps a radio host asks, "How can our listeners get more information on what you have to offer?" Your answer to that question must telegraph value. People value their time, so they'd want to know whether the call would be valuable to them even if you're giving consultations for free.

Consider creating a secondary call to action for those not ready to talk to a live person. Remember, the people prepared to make a phone call are typically already in the market. We mentioned earlier in the book that these people make up only 3% of the market. The rest are either in information-gathering mode or even earlier in the cycle.

I'll give you a sample answer from my DJ business. I would say: "If somebody wants to talk to a full-time entertainer right now, specifically about a date they have coming up, they can call me at 555-1212, or they can download my free report, *What Every Young Bride Needs to Know About Wedding Entertainment* at www. website.com."

Here's a bonus tip: If you offer a free consultation, you should give it a unique name so it sounds different from everybody else's complimentary offer. For example, I call my free consultation in my DJ business "A Dream Wedding Reception Discovery Call." And I will briefly describe what we will do in that call so they can picture it in their minds, and it will compel them to make the appointment.

Trust Trigger #5: The Status Effect

The most overriding factor for whether someone decides to take your offer is how they think they will appear to others around them, including family, friends, colleagues, or peers. People don't like to admit it, but most are self-conscious and care more about what others think of them than what they think about themselves. Will this investment raise or lower their status immediately? They're thinking, "How long will it take to get my results, and how will I look in the meantime?" They ask themselves, "How do I rationalize this investment to myself or my spouse? Is this a risk to my status? What happens if this doesn't work? Will hiring this person bring status or embarrass me? Are they an author or locally known, perhaps even a celebrity?"

An example question from a radio host could be: "What kind of results can folks expect?" Your answers can be the real benefits of your service or products, and a subtle mention of your guarantee telegraphs protection of their status. You have to make them believe that they can undo the problem if anything goes south and not look foolish to their peers or family.

The status effect also allows you to point out that they would be working with a leading expert in the field. For example, if you're an author of a book on a subject, that creates a positive halo effect of working with a leading expert. Can you see how that would increase your prospect's status with peers and family?

Here are some action steps from this chapter:

1. Start by making a list in two columns. You can do this with your word-processing software or with an old-school notebook.

2. On the left side of the page, list the five trust triggers, and on the right side, brainstorm a list of examples you can add to your messaging, addressing each one. This is an

exercise you can do with your team and can be an excellent reference for creating content for videos, interviews, and social media.

3. Expand this list to create a content inventory that will become your go-to source.

KEY TAKEAWAYS

> Always address all five trust triggers when communicating with your target audience.

> Don't just say your trust trigger answers; demonstrate them with stories or case studies of past clients.

> Constantly rehearse your origin story and pack it with trust triggers. Make a habit of shortening, condensing, and tightening your origin story until you internalize it.

> Identify the stories and case studies you should use for your brand by listing the trust triggers and brainstorming examples. Keep refining these until your trust trigger messages are compact, powerful, straightforward, and easy to remember.

ActionBrand Marketing Assets aka The Prime Positioning Portfolio

"The simple truth is, if you aren't deliberately, systematically, methodically — or rapidly and dramatically — establishing yourself as a celebrity at least to your clientele and target market, you're asleep at the wheel, ignoring what is fueling the entire economy around you, neglecting the development of a measurably valuable asset."

DAN KENNEDY

Now that we've discussed the types of customers and clients you want to attract and work with and clarified the messages you want to send, it's time to cover the vehicles you will use to deliver your messages.

In ActionBranding, I call this your **"Prime Positioning Portfolio."**

Great News!

In today's age, it's incredibly easy and suspiciously cheap to promote your business and be seen in a positive light. With the quality of cameras and cell phones today, you have everything you need to craft content in your pocket.

In this brief chapter, we'll go over the basic core items you can use to position yourself effectively using ActionBranding to drive fast sales and accelerated acceptance by anchoring your company in the minds of your prospects.

With the amount of free and near-free media platforms available online, you can reach everyone right in their pocket via cell phone.

There are many different media and methods for getting your message out to the world. Within the scope of this chapter, I want to give you the essentials. Let's look at it as the minimum effective dose. This way, once you've built your brand marketing foundation, it will be easy to add more. You can experiment with advanced methods, but let's ensure you have these fundamentals down first. This is about creating a significant, growing footprint online with all roads leading back to you.

When ActionBranding your company, there are two things for you to consider.

1. Be a Google Darling

When people Google your name, you want good stuff to show up. Period.

No matter what you do or how well you present to someone, they are doing their due diligence. If they hear about you, they will type your name in Google. If they are referred to you even by close friends, they type your name into Google.

The idea here is you want to ensure that the right things appear when people research you. That could be the tipping point that ticks all the boxes for all the trust triggers we discussed in the previous chapter.

2. People Look For Answers, Not Advertising

People are already searching for answers to their problems. They're typing questions into Google. They're searching YouTube, the second largest search engine online. ActionBrand Marketing is based on Direct-Response Marketing; therefore, all your marketing assets and video titles are problem/solution-based rather than company or product-based.

Origin Stories

These stories are assets that should be collected, cataloged, and categorized for your consistent reference use in future marketing assets. I mean documenting stories around you, your business, and your solution to problems you solve that support what your brand stands for.

Over time, as people become familiar with your brand, there are things you want them to know. You want them to know who you stand for and what enemies you stand against. You want them to know how you came to be the advocate and educator for the success of your clients and customers.

If you had a childhood incident that led you on a lifelong quest that eventually became your business, document that story. Take all the Trust Triggers discussed in the previous chapter and see if you have real stories in your history that support any of those triggers.

Take the author of "Rich Dad, Poor Dad," Robert Kiyosaki, for a real-life example. His origin story is telegraphed right in his book title. He explains that he became an advocate for financial and entrepreneurial literacy because he grew up figuratively with two dads. His own dad was his "poor dad," a professor who earned a lot yet struggled financially. His friend's dad left school early and became an entrepreneur and one of the wealthiest men in Hawaii.

Kiyosaki's origin story explains how he studied both dads' perspectives and how the rich dad's advice gave him the knowledge of finances to gain wealth.

People understand stories and remember stories better than facts alone. For that reason, make it a priority to catalog stories in your business.

Your Signature Book

People are also searching Amazon for products and solutions to their problems. Amazon is like a search engine for buyers. It is similar to how nobody goes into a restaurant to browse; people go to Amazon intending to buy something to scratch an itch.

Guess what? That's why we are going to put out a signature book.

Imagine how valuable it would be to have a signature book appear on Amazon when somebody searches your name on Google. Imagine if this signature book telegraphs a solution to your ideal client's most common, pressing problems. For example, if you're a wedding entertainer, imagine your book title is "How to Create the Ultimate Wedding Reception."

People on Google searching for solutions to problems are looking to escape pain, learn new things, or aspire to some next level. Think of the terms your ideal prospects will be typing into

Google. What are they looking for? What questions are they asking? Brainstorm titles you can create for your book.

Books are my favorite, most overlooked, best-kept secret to growing your business or brand. In today's trust-based economy, there's no greater tool for building trust than demonstrating your ability and passion to help.

Books are amazing shortcuts that help people quickly understand and recognize who you are. We will go over this in more detail in the chapter on The Nucleus of Your ActionBranding, your signature book.

The Fallacy of "What You Do" Marketing

Some of the earliest ways to promote yourself online were using SEO keyword-loaded terms like "Houston Weight Loss" or "Best Naperville Dentist."

Nothing wrong with owning those terms. But how valuable are they?

When somebody types "Best Naperville Dentist," unfortunately, you and about 100 of your closest competitors will appear in the search term context. It only allows you to deliver a generic tour of your business and somehow differentiate yourself or get them to believe you're the best *like everybody else.* That's sarcasm.

What is another option?

Use "Who You Are" Marketing

As I mentioned, having those SEO keyword-loaded terms going into your content is okay. However, it would be more valuable if you added additional content focusing on who you are and who you serve in a way that addresses the five trust triggers we discussed in the previous chapter.

Instead of using the headline or titling your video "Houston Weight Loss," call it "Safest Weight Loss Method" to attract people searching for the safest weight loss method. This allows you to deliver an education-based video, sharing the safest weight loss method and how it differs from other methods. Because you are providing the information, it is already implied that you are the expert in that method.

Rather than competing like a commodity, you can demonstrate your expertise by answering the most common questions and sharing pearls of wisdom by sharing answers to questions they didn't even think to ask. These make for eye-opening content videos. You automatically will be seen as the obvious expert when you share this information.

As a reminder of the trust triggers, you will be able to address Affinity, which is, "Do you understand my problem?" The Provider, which asks, "Are you qualified to help me?" The Method, which asks, "Why is your method the right one for me?" The

Value Proposition, which asks, "Is this a good value? What will I get from this compared to other options? And what is the result compared to other options for the money invested?" Finally, you can address the Status trust trigger, which asks, "How will I look good by working with you, and what do I risk if all goes bad?"

Consistent Video Content

The public's attention span today is both a blessing and a curse. The curse is people are so inundated by information that they look for shortcuts to what to pay attention to. They need the content to be brief, concise, and to the point. The good news is that you can create short content.

You can create one long piece of content with several topics strung together. This allows you to repurpose your video by having an editor slice it into multiple parts. This makes it easier for you to produce marketing materials. Set a "video shoot day" monthly and create content for the entire month. This video content can be repurposed on several different platforms.

YouTube Channel

YouTube is one of the most valuable and effective gifts given to you by the Internet. Youtube channels are free to create, and because Google owns YouTube, it ranks very highly on Google's search engine.

If you want to run an experiment, create a short video, title it with your name and company name, and post it on YouTube. Type your name or company name into Google within weeks, and see what happens. Use this power to create video titles matching questions that people will ask.

Once you've created a video for YouTube, you can repurpose it and post it on other social media platforms like Facebook, LinkedIn, Snapchat, Instagram, Tiktok, or whatever video or social media platforms may be popular when you read this book.

Another great benefit of marketing videos is that you can strip out their audio tracks and use them for a podcast that can appear on Apple, Spotify, Audible, or other platforms users download podcasts from.

Be cautious about your time. I prefer not to get too carried away with new platforms until you see traction because they can be a black hole. After all, social media platforms do come and go. In recent memory, before Facebook Live took off, there was Periscope. I don't think people will even remember that anymore. At the beginning of the pandemic, everybody was yammering about Clubhouse. I haven't heard a word about that platform in a long time.

You'll hear gurus like Gary Vee say that social media is free, so be everywhere. But you must be cautious because his "free" social media costs him tens of thousands of dollars in salaries each month for his team to help him "be everywhere." It will either cost you your time or somebody else's time that you pay for. Let's remember that. That's why I'm sharing the minimum effective dose here.

Using Interviews as Content

Talk radio-style interviews are one of my favorite business formats because people are so conditioned to love interviews. People love watching Oprah and Dr. Phil. The format of questions from the host and answers from the guest expert is so anchored in the public's mind that it makes presenting the most complicated information easy to grasp for the listener.

One of the tricks I used when I was on terrestrial radio was to theme our episodes according to whatever I wanted to promote within the coming weeks. We would do the show and deliver the content with the intention of repurposing the entire show as an audio infomercial. We would take the audios of the show and deliver them in MP3 and, (I'm dating myself here) even on CDs, to promote current offers. Every time you do a show, you have an asset. If your content is evergreen, you could use it for years to come.

Another great thing about creating a radio show or podcast is life is a moving parade. These formats allow you to tie your message to current events, deliver value, and show up regularly in people's lives in a meaningful and impactful way. One of the best ways to keep your ActionBrand relevant is by interviewing guest experts and other complementary experts that can serve your audience. You also get the opportunity to build strong referral partnerships with your guests.

Get Yourself on Network Television

You can get interviewed on influential platforms. Start somewhere; even start with a local channel where their logo will appear on the video that gives you that extra endorsement. Level up from there. You can send those local segments to more extensive local networks like ABC, NBC, and FOX to show them you are a capable and logical guest option for their show.

There are ways to sponsor segments on those larger local networks. Just do it. These videos are priceless when you use them for your content and repurpose them on YouTube and all of your platforms. Plus, you can deliberately drive traffic to these videos with paid advertising.

Articles and Blogs

The videos you have already created can be transcribed into blog articles. They could stay in interview format, or you can have them rewritten and turned into first-person. Articles and blogs also have headlines just like your videos' titles, which can help your content rank higher for more traffic from Google and other search engines.

Magazine Tear Sheets

You can turn your articles into good-looking magazine tear sheets and other print material. Please note that you're not trying to fool people with this type of content. But just like a radio interview makes it easier for people to understand the format, people are accustomed to seeing magazines on the newsstand.

Have your articles turned into mini magazines with your photo on the front cover. Get your article titles on the cover just like Cosmopolitan magazine would.

Again, we're not trying to fool people. We're simply presenting information in an entertaining way that makes people want to read and, most importantly, anchor your ActionBrand in their minds.

Since you are creating a mock magazine, you can create a magazine name that telegraphs or matches the audience you want to attract. For example, if you are a wedding entertainer, your magazine can be called "Remarkable Receptions."

Press Releases

All your content can be transcribed and announced using a press release sent to the media. For example, suppose you interview a specific guest on your show. In that case, you can have a press release with the headline "Special Guest (insert their name)

Discusses *How to Make Your Wedding Memorable and Fun* on Remarkable Radio." Within the body of the press release, you could link to the full video, audio, or podcast.

Next, send your PR to as many press release distribution platforms as possible. Send your releases to hundreds of media channels. When you receive the report back, you'll potentially see hundreds of links to your site. You also get access to hundreds of articles you can screenshot or drive prospects to.

When people stumble upon these articles, they read your content and can click your link, driving them to the original interview, where you can have a call to action and get people to subscribe. See how you build a spiderweb, capturing people at every turn and drawing them into your tractor beam?

Newsletter

A must-have for every business and private practice professional is a newsletter you send regularly to your audience, typically monthly. This staple of consistent communication with your customers, clients, and prospects keeps you top-of-mind in your category and community. Your newsletter should be in print. At a minimum, you could send an email newsletter.

Your newsletter's content should contain topics of interest to your audience and NOT just about your business! For example, if you have an auto shop in a particular town, your newsletter columns could have a community calendar and things to do for families with kids. If you want your newsletter read, you don't want to only write about tune-ups and tire rotations. Make it fun, like something you'd like to receive from a friend, not just a business.

At a minimum, send your newsletter to the list you build. Further, depending on your economics, you can send it to your prospective audience to add more names to your list.

Video Newsletter

Coming from a disc jockey background, as a tech geek, I was on top of online video since before YouTube. I learned how to get videos online from Jim Edwards and Mike Stewart in their course, Website Video Secrets, and I was hooked. I sent emails to my list that had links to web pages where I hosted my videos. Nowadays, YouTube and cheap video hosting abound, and you can send videos to your audience.

What I like about the video newsletter is that we can economically send it weekly for better, top-of-mind touches because it is online. The content is just like the print newsletter, a mix of tips, tricks, and secrets that benefit your audience, not limited to just being about your business. Any relevant offer or invitation can be given with each video newsletter email.

Something I have pioneered for my clients is the weekly Video Newsletter. We film the month's episodes in one session and take care of all the tech, so our clients simply schedule a weekly email to their list that contains the episodes. We mix audience-relevant topics, interviews with referral partners, and community news, making it feel like a fun weekly touch from a friend.

The coolest part about the video newsletter is that we compile the separate weekly topics into the monthly print version deliverable. Any coupons or offers are included in the print newsletter. This gives you more bang for your buck and guaranteed top-of-mind with your fans and audience.

Traditional Brand Assets aka Tangible Brand Assets

Notice how I saved "traditional brand assets" (T-shirts and baseball caps with your logo on them) for last? There's nothing wrong with these items. They play a significant supporting role in ActionBranding. But, you should give and make them available to already converted fans. Once people have decided that you are the obvious expert in your company, which is the one they love, you then use your logo and image to anchor your company in their minds.

This is where you offer these branded materials to your already converted prospects, clients, and customers. It gives them the ability to express themselves through your brand.

At the end of the day, people want a brand they can rally around — something that represents them and their beliefs.

Like attracts like, and it is your job to create raving fans.

In the next chapter, you will discover the key elements of your tangible brand assets.

The ActionBranding Anchor in the Mind

Everything you create is intended to plant a specific thought seed in the mind of your prospects. This applies to every piece of content you develop. For example, it can introduce you as the best-selling author of your signature book. The title of your book telegraphs the problems you solved and how you solved them, as well as the aspirations you help your clients achieve.

When you appear in videos, be thoughtful about the setting. If you have awards related to your work, be sure they are subtly placed in the background of the video. Have your best-selling book on display behind you.

Every piece of content should plant a specific seed. Included in those seeds is that you are an accomplished expert in your field, an educator, an advocate, perhaps an award winner and that you are busy, in-demand, and popular.

You do not need their money, but you are happy to help if they are the right client for you.

Also, in your videos or podcasts, the guest experts you feature telegraph that you work with the best. It shows that you have your audience's best interest in mind, and the focus is not always on you but on other people you know will help them.

If you're just starting out, pick only one medium and go all-in on it. Don't spread yourself thin by trying to be on every platform. If you feel you are a better writer than a talker, write blog articles. Do a podcast or radio show if you're better at talking than writing. If you're good on camera, do a video podcast and a YouTube channel. Gain traction with one medium before you add another. Scale your media as you scale your business so your effort is sustainable.

KEY TAKEAWAYS

> Establish a compelling "Prime Positioning Portfolio" for effective ActionBranding.

> Secure a positive online presence for credibility when people search your name.

> Prioritize education-based content that addresses problems and questions.

> Share origin stories and connect them to your brand's values.

> Create a signature book to showcase expertise and solutions.

> Focus on identity-driven marketing over generic keyword-based strategies.

> Craft concise video content that can be repurposed across platforms.

> Utilize YouTube for visibility and higher search engine ranking.

> Send a video and print newsletter regularly to your audience to stay top-of-mind.

> Leverage interviews to provide valuable content and build trust.

> Network TV appearances can significantly boost your credibility.

> Go all-in on one channel before posting on all platforms.

Tangible Branding Asset Basics

"Products are made in the factory, but brands
are created in the mind."

WALTER LANDOR, LANDOR & FITCH

For many who are new to starting a business or working for themselves, the tangible assets of branding are where they gravitate first. Until they learn that their brand's "look and feel" is less important in the beginning than actionable offers and clarified messaging, too many folks unknowingly invest all their energy and resources in this area only to find it doesn't produce results in the bank on its own.

However, there are some basics to consider, such as a "name," because it will follow you for a lifetime, and you will invest resources to build it. So, this name better be timeless and unconfining rather than trendy and limiting.

At its core, branding is about creating a unique identity, similar to a human personality, for a product, service, or company. This identity should resonate with your ideal audience, differentiate from the competition, and even repel less-than-ideal audiences.

While branding involves a wide variety of elements that I have discussed throughout this book, the scope of this particular chapter focuses solely on the basics of the tangible, sensory aspects of your brand that you can experience with the five senses, such as see and feel. These include your logo, colors, and other physical brand representations. This is quite a broad topic, so consider this chapter merely an overview.

The Main Objective Behind the Tangible Brand Assets

Tangible brand assets are the visual and physical manifestation of a brand's identity. For example, if you look at a brand as a "person," how does that person express themselves? That person will have a style, a look, a personality, and a smell. They will dress a certain way, speak a certain way, and act a certain way. Those attributes will likely be congruent with who they are at their core. We want to view our brand and, therefore, our brand assets similarly.

People attach these physical elements to other humans and anchor their views of them in their minds. As they get to know a person and observe their style and behaviors, they begin to form their perception of them. This is similar to how the world gets to know a brand. So, you must craft all the elements of your brand to be congruent with its core values. Think of what your logo, colors, and style express to the world.

However, make no mistake that a logo alone will mean nothing *until* it is anchored into your audience's mind. The Nike™ swoosh logo may mean something to you today, but if it were not for billions of dollars spent over decades anchoring the brand in the public's mind, the swoosh would be an invisible scribble. Do you have this budget or time to wait? This concept is lost among many, leading to wasted resources and time creating imagery rather than a clear message and offer.

Key Tangible Brand Assets:

- **Logo**
- **Colors**
- **Business Card**
- **Product and Service Packaging**
- **Experiential**

Let's take a closer look at each.

The Power of a Logo

Your logo is the foundational element of recognition. Over time, the look of your logo can anchor your brand into your audience's mind. That is why this element is important. Your logo can be a shape (like the Nike™ swoosh), the words of your brand in a unique style font, or a combination of both.

Simplicity, Memorability, and Relevance

Your logo should have a balance of simplicity and distinctiveness. It should have the ability to be quickly distinguished and recognized. Consider your industry, the type of people in your audience, and what is attractive to them when choosing a look and feel for your logo.

Shape Considerations

Different shapes convey different emotions and messages and can differ among cultures. When I say "shape," I refer to the shape you may choose for a symbol (if you decide to have one) and the overall shape of your logo, including the words.

For example, logos, including or laid out in circular or oval shapes, are used by brands to convey unity, longevity, and trust.

Square and rectangular layouts or logo shapes convey stability and reliability. Corporations prefer these shapes to convey strength, structure, and dependability.

A triangular layout or shape can convey innovation, growth, or movement. You will see this a lot in technology and construction.

Organic shapes and layouts express nature, harmony, and approachability, whereas abstract shapes can convey a feeling of modernness and creativity (if not weirdness). Brands that want to appear avant-garde or rebellious can choose an abstract image.

Also, consider how the shape of your logo will transfer across different media. For example, one of my early brands had a symbol and words, and when I sponsored an event, the logo became unreadable when placed among all the sponsors on a webpage. The lesson I learned for my purpose was that words are more important than symbols, so I adjusted my view accordingly. Take this into consideration. If your logo, even if it is just words, sits like a long rectangle, it will be shrunk when put online among other logos that are set square. In my experience, balancing your logo width and height will be more adaptable.

Versatility

When I think about logos, I always ask, "Will this logo look good on merchandise?" (t-shirts, hats, etc). Will it swag? How will your logo transfer to websites, social platforms, and print materials?

Timelessness

Avoid trendy styles, fonts, or clever misspellings. Choose a style that will stand the test of time. New research in The Journal of Marketing revealed that consumers dislike cleverly misspelled or unconventionally spelled names like Lyft and Tumblr. It could help you secure an available domain name. However, the juice may not be worth the squeeze. Researchers caution new brands against misspelled names to appear young, hip, or trendy as you can become outdated quickly.

Color Psychology

In branding, the choice of color speaks volumes about a brand's style and personality, even before a single word or message is made or understood.

Audience Alignment

Color choice should reflect the audience that you serve and the industry you are in. Consider how John Deere™ chose the color green. Research shows a positive association between green and nature and regrowth, making it a strong choice of brand color for a manufacturer of agricultural, construction, and forestry equipment.

Another layer of thought should be put into how the color translates culturally. For example, purple could mean royalty and luxury in some countries, but how will it translate globally? If your business is not global, that may not be a concern.

Emotional Resonance

Another consideration in color choice is how the color makes people feel. There are countless books and references regarding emotions elicited by specific colors. For example, blue is a safe choice that many companies make because of the trustworthy, good feeling it creates. Researchers surmise it is because a blue sky and water are perceived as good signs.

A sports brand may choose the color red for its expression of strength and power. Think about why red is the stereotypical color of a sports car.

Recognition & Differentiation

When you are first in a field, you have the key to the castle. When you are second or later, you need to consider your competition. In an area rife with competition, consider what colors are already taken, which can guide you to finding a differentiator. Interestingly, while John Deere™ owned the color green in the market, their biggest competitor, International Harvester™, became famously known for their red-colored tractors because

Deere struggled to enter the tractor market then. However, in the end, John Deere™ prevailed and won the tractor war. Which brand is more of a household name, John Deere™ or Case IH (International Harvester)™? Which one do YOU resonate with most? Do you think color had anything to do with it? On a side note, my better half, Shannon, is a John Deere™ fangirl owning hats and t-shirts of the brand, and we have landscapers, so she never touches a blade of grass or dirt, let alone cooks!

Examples In Action

Tiffany & Co. uses a shade of light blue associated with luxury and exclusivity. All gift-givers know the emotions they evoke by merely presenting the box.

McDonald's™ beat other hamburger fast-food chains to the colors yellow and red, which stimulate appetite and attract attention. This makes picking a color more challenging for the next burger joint. Hence, look at the Burger King™ colors, as they used natural shades reflecting their bread, meat, and vegetables. It's not as appealing, in my humble opinion.

Business Card

Even in today's digital age, the printed business card remains vital to professional and personal branding. It is a tangible anchor of a personal interaction and a quick way to share contact information.

Your business card is an excellent opportunity to add another branding touchpoint compactly.

For the same reason I believe in physical books over digital ebooks (and you should have both), you must have a physical business card, not just a digital one.

When I sponsor a booth at a conference, out of hundreds of visitors to my booth, one or two folks only have a "digital" business card with a QR code. No matter what they believe is in the power of their digital business card, take it from me; the old curmudgeon on the receiving end of that card thinks it's a pain in the ass!

When I'm presented with that card, I smile and point my camera at their QR code, and most of the time, their contact info gets lost in digital oblivion. Is it in my phone? Maybe. Is it where I have systematically put my contacts for that particular show? Definitely NOT. That is just one user experience example of why fancy schmancy digital business cards won't replace having a real one. Your digital card may be helpful for casual interactions, so have both. But please have a physical business card as your primary.

Designing Your Business Card

Be sure your card reflects your colors, logo, and typeface. Include your essential contact information, such as name, title, company, email, website URL, and phone number, in an easy-to-see way. Optionally, include your core social handles, but don't overdo it.

To stand out, consider unique materials, shapes, or custom printing methods, such as watermarks, that can add a lasting impression.

Your business card often makes the first impression, so be sure it is well-designed and professionally printed. It will telegraph a level of credibility (or lack thereof) and attention to detail.

I carry separate cards for my radio show, and each business has its own card. I have a different card for Books Grow Business and Imperial Action. My Books Grow Business card features the cover of my book of the same name as the front of the card, and the contact information is all on the back. That's a cool benefit of being a published author because your book already brands you in your audience's mind, and the card quickly offers another anchor.

Product and Service Packaging

Whether your business provides products or services, they come with "packaging." In a product business, the products are delivered in some sort of package. In a service business, that "packaging" is expressed in the words, web page, video, or print used to sell it.

With the advent of internet video and social media, "unboxing videos" became a thing. This is a gift to every product business on the planet because it offers an opportunity to create a great unboxing experience. How can you make your product look as good to unbox as it is to use?

Considerations for packaging a product should include type of material, shape, on-brand colors, and congruence with your brand and audience. For example, is your brand eco-friendly, and are you using eco-friendly materials?

Selling a service on a website should grab attention. Besides the brand name of the service or package, how are the design, colors, and user experience enhancing the desirability and consumption of your message?

Experiential Marketing

My earliest experience with big brands started in Experiential Marketing or Engagement Marketing. This approach invites consumers or your ideal audience to participate with your brand or product. The strategy focuses on creating interactive, memorable, and shareable experiences between your audience and your brand or products.

I was hired to travel to Baltimore to create and play the soundtrack for Under Armour's surprise announcement of its first shoe line in

2006. This event was being held not for consumers but for their international sales force. The goal was to fire up the entire Under Armour culture and its sales team. We started with the traditional fashion show for each sport, such as golf, basketball, and soccer. Then, as the energy rose to a choreographed crescendo, Kevin Plank appeared to make the monumental announcement of the first Under Armour shoe line. Experiential works in B2B and B2C with any audience you want to engage.

Interactive Experience

Brands would hire me to design and deploy an interactive, experiential event to generate publicity and buzz to stay relevant. I've been the emcee host of The Pokémon Worlds event in Hawaii. I've been the ring announcer for Nintendo's Super Smash Brothers Brawl game launch tour, which was themed as a national championship tournament with events in Chicago, Los Angeles, San Francisco, Boston, and NYC.

I also deployed a product launch event for the Nintendo DS handheld and Nintendo's Nintendogs game. The event theme was a "doggie fashion show" launch party in Battery Park in New York City, where my team spent the prior week passing out invitations all over NYC. At the party, my DJ team entertained the crowd with follow-along dances and music that set the tone to bring the guest of honor to the stage. The crowd was surprised and delighted to meet the esteemed Mr. Shigeru Miyamoto, creator of the Nintendogs game, who also created Donkey Kong and The Legend of Zelda, among other loved games. The audience received a surprise gift bag with the Nintendo DS console and the Nintendogs game! Even more remarkable, we announced that the audience could power up their game and engage with a then-popular guest celebrity, Hillary Duff's Nintendog! We had many photo opportunities, and attendees had plenty to share on social media, so mission accomplished. This event created the buzz, publicity, and news that spread like wildfire and drove fans to retail!

Mark with Nintendo's Shigeru Miyamoto at Battery Park NYC at the launch party for the Nintendo DS game Nintendogs

Instead of demonstrating or presenting a product or service, you create a hands-on, immersive experience where your audience can participate. These experiences can be delivered through sampling, events, installations, pop-ups, or gamified demonstrations, among other methods.

The more you match the event to the audience, location, and relevance, the more attention and buzz you can create.

These interactions should evoke an emotional response, whether happiness, exhilaration, curiosity, or even shock and awe. I have witnessed firsthand the power of these emotional engagements and how they create stronger bonds between the consumer and the brand.

What's cool about Experiential Marketing is that it is designed as an "event," encouraging attendees to share their experiences and leveraging social media to amplify the event further.

You measure the impact of Experiential Marketing from the social media buzz, brand awareness growth, or even sales. As ActionBrand Marketers, we keep this in the context of exponential growth. When done well, these events could be imagined as sales opportunities. Although the big brands don't typically direct-sell at these events because they are bolstering their brand to drive consumers to retailers, an idea for ActionBranders is to make direct sales on-site.

For example, in the mid-90s, when I sold pet iguanas at the flea market, my booth featured "Pet the giant iguana on your shoulder." We also offered a Polaroid picture keepsake for sale as the gimmick, but we focused on letting people hold the iguana for free, so we got maximum traffic and attention at our booth. My booth sold tons of baby pet iguanas that way. It may be a strange thought, but nobody carried a camera back then, and if I had to do it today, I believe it would work even better!

Brand Consistency and Cohesion

Since the branding part of ActionBrand Marketing is the long game, you must stick to a consistent and cohesive look and feel to build a memorable and recognizable brand. This way, no matter how someone interacts with your brand, they get a unified experience. Every time you go on a date with the same person, do they act like themselves, dress the way you expect, or even smell the same? Again, an easy way to always be on brand is to think of your brand as a person so you could more easily filter how it would look, feel, and act if it were human.

There is a lot more to learn about the tangible assets of a brand, so this chapter was meant to give you a solid foundational overview of the basics.

KEY TAKEAWAYS

> Tangible brand assets are essential in building a memorable brand identity alongside messaging and offers. These include logos, colors, and business cards, all contributing to the brand's visual and sensory impact.

> The design of the logo is key to brand recognition. It should balance simplicity with distinctiveness, be versatile across different media, and avoid fleeting trends for a timeless appeal.

> Color choice in branding should reflect the brand's audience and industry and consider emotional resonance and the need to stand out from competitors.

> Despite the rise of digital media, physical business cards remain vital to professional branding, offering a direct and personal way to share contact information and reinforce brand identity.

> Effective product and service packaging and engaging Experiential Marketing enhance the customer's interaction with the brand, creating memorable experiences and telegraphing brand values.

> Place importance on the tangible brand assets; however, know that they won't make sales on their own. Therefore, don't spend a disproportionate amount of resources on them, and don't let them overshadow the importance of a clear message and direct response offers.

Marketing Your Offers

"The confused mind takes no action."

- MARK IMPERIAL

This chapter provides a streamlined way to get your offers out into the world, which is the quickest path to a sale. Although the readers of this book are from many different industries and business niches, the principles of marketing their offers remain the same.

I always say as ActionBranders; we are professional explainers. Our advertisements are drenched in education. We believe in education-based marketing. In the term ActionBrand, the word "Action" is first. This means direct response is the key. No slogans or clever taglines are needed.

You will address your prospects' pains and offer your content as the solution and payoff for reading or watching. You will get them to consume your content to gain their trust and ask them to engage. Engagement can be in the form of booking an appointment or a consultation with you or purchasing a low-ticket solution. Of course, we test each engagement type to determine the best path.

These are the five elements to create an ActionBrand Marketing Funnel:

1. Your ActionBrand DNA
2. Your Irresistible Offer
3. Your ActionBrand Lead Page
4. Your Signature ActionBrand Website
5. Your Nurturing Campaign Formula

Here's the breakdown:

1. Your ActionBrand DNA

You've been working on your message. You want the world to know what you're about. Take the message you created from the "ActionBrand DNA" chapter, and integrate it everywhere in your materials. I mention this again because this message rides on top of everything else we're going to do in promoting your offers. Every message or every piece of content has to telegraph bits and pieces and elements of your DNA because it is the personality of your company and your personal brand.

2. Your Irresistible Offer

In ActionBranding, there will always be an irresistible offer. We won't be wasting money or anchoring otherwise meaningless terms like "the real thing" or "the choice of a new generation." By the way, what brands are anchored with those phrases? After hundreds of millions of dollars spent, I hope you would know that those slogans belong to Coke and Pepsi, respectively. The critical thing to note is: Did those taglines get you to buy?

In contrast, ActionBrand Marketing asks you to take action. To get your prospect to take action, you need an irresistible, specific offer regarding what you want them to do.

Lead Magnets, AKA Free Offers for Lead Generation

"Lead magnets" are free offers to entice your prospect to give you their contact information. Such offers are called lead magnets because they attract people to provide you with their information and become one of your leads.

Some examples of lead magnets are PDFs or white papers, perhaps tickets to a live event or dinner seminar, or a webinar invitation. A lead magnet can be an invitation to register for a free video or video series or a free sample, or, one of my favorites, a book. These media promise solutions to prospects' most burning problems.

In the mid-1990s, when email was new, I jokingly used it as a simple offer when I saw a girl in an oil change place while waiting for my car. All I had to say was, "Hey! Let's exchange email addresses!" Just the novelty of being one of the few people with an email address at that time made getting contacts easy. Not anymore! Email is one of the most widely abused media on the planet and is now the most highly protected and guarded media. You have to offer high value and be trustworthy to get people's email addresses today.

The most common free offer for lead generation and often the most effective, depending on the type of business promoted, is information such as white papers, guides, and books that answer your audience's most pressing questions.

At this point, I need to clarify that you can't take free offers for granted. You might be thinking that it's easy to give something away. But you would be surprised to find that it could be just as difficult to sell a free offer as it is to sell a paid offer. After all, the scarcest resource on the planet is personal time, and people are very protective of their time. It's the one thing that nobody can ever replace. You can replace money, but you cannot replace time. Not surprisingly, most people won't put up with your shenanigans just because you're offering something for free.

If you can trigger a fascination about your company and solution and your prospect truly believes you can help them thrive, they will want to stay connected with you and hear from you. This should be your goal. Strive to build a list of interested prospects.

It begins with researching your audience so deeply that you know what they are already buying, what they are already interested in, and what they are already requesting. One of the easiest ways to do this is to look at your competitors and see what they offer. Can you find a gap that you can exploit? Can you add something to what your competitors are already offering to make it better? Can you come up with something more valuable than what your competitors thought of offering?

In the early 2000s, I built my DJs Edge coaching business to help fellow DJs improve the marketing of their businesses. I offered a free CD titled "How I Went From a Dead Broke, Dime-A-Dozen DJ to Make Over $167,500 in Just 12 Months as a Single Operator and How You Can Too."

You have to know that I was speaking to a very specific audience in a very specific language. Wedding and mobile DJs who work solo know the term "single operator." The kind of money I mentioned is shocking to 95% of single operators because they typically only work on Saturday nights.

To make six figures for a part-time job is quite surprising for that audience, so the CD was requested by thousands of DJ entertainers, and hundreds of them became paying coaching clients of mine. Many attended my events and even became recurring monthly members. My CD giveaway offer allowed me to build a high six-figure part-time coaching business. Without that CD offer, the business wouldn't have existed.

Ways to Uncover Your Irresistible Offer

Ask yourself these questions:

- What transformation do you offer?
- Can you provide for free the first step of a full range of services or products you have?
- Can you give away the floor plan so the prospect would want the blueprint?

The principle behind this is that people need the floor plan to see the big picture of what you are offering, especially if it is unique to them. The floor plan sample gets them so excited that they now want the step-by-step guide in which you can sell them the blueprint. Can you give them something for free that would create the desire to purchase the rest? One example is a 12-module video course where you give away the first video, enticing them to want to join or buy the rest of the course.

THIS IS ACTIONBRAND MARKETING

Think about how a photographer at a school dance takes a bunch of pictures for free, shows them to you with a puppy dog close, and, if you like the pics, offers you the prints to buy.

Offers for Purchase

Take a lesson from mail-order houses. When I was a kid, my favorite advertisement on the back of comic books was the Johnson Smith ad. They would advertise one or two gimmicks like rubber dog poop, sneezing power, or other fun pranks. Their advertisements would start by offering only their most popular product. Then, once you purchase the product, they will mail you their entire catalog along with an offer for the next most popular product. Their offer got me hooked. I remember staying up all night going through every page of their catalog and circling all the nonsense items I wanted to buy next.

This is the key idea behind making an offer for purchase. Think about your best-selling item or service. Can you make a low-ticket sampler item out of something that is currently your most popular service? Think about how that can be part of the stepladder of products or services, or what I like to call "a family of products or services," that you can offer sequentially.

Make yourself a visual graphic of a wheel. What would your best customer own in that wheel in a perfect world? Would they want to own the whole thing? If so, what would get them started, and what would naturally be the next step?

3. Your ActionBrand Lead Page

When I first learned about these pages, they were referred to as mini-sites. Today, people refer to them as landing or squeeze pages. These are different from a typical website because they are built for one thing only: capturing page visitors' information to build your mailing list. These pages focus only on one problem, offer one solution, and feature one call to action. The idea behind a landing page is that it would match the advertisement that sent ad clickers to that page.

For instance, if you offer an insomnia cure and tell people to go to a specific webpage, they would click through, and the page would greet visitors with a message that telegraphs that you were glad they made it. It will then talk about the insomnia cure information they are looking for. The webpage would include information about your system, testimonials, and relevant case studies. Still, it would only ask the visitor to do one thing and one thing alone: enter their email or contact information to receive the promised information.

As an illustration, if you created the insomnia cure ad and sent prospects to an ActionBrand webpage that described the insomnia problem and offered the free, digital version of the book on the insomnia cure just by entering the email address, that is where it would end.

Now, to view the big picture, let's say your company is a hypnosis business, and you cure many different ailments, including smoking. You may address weight loss; perhaps insomnia is one of the issues tackled. Well, the "one problem, one solution" funnel spoke to page visitors with insomnia specifically without mention of anything else that you cure. The time to disclose everything you do is after you've captured them as an interested prospect, and even then, it may be wise to discuss your other cures way later in the funnel. You need to speak to these people about their specific problems only for a while.

4. Your Signature ActionBrand Website

Now it's time to create a signature website encompassing your entire business and core services. This will be your main website, but not one you promote directly from your ads.

Like the Johnson Smith catalog example I mentioned above, this website is only shown to people already converted into prospects or first-purchase buyers of your most popular products or services. The website should be shown to your buyers to cross-promote your other services if relevant. Sending them to this page first may not be the best path because it doesn't allow you to present your services in the order in which you want them to be seen.

The most intelligent path is one doorway using the previous description of an ActionBrand Lead Page. Your business can have multiple single doors, but send them to the individual doorways before you present your core website.

5. Your Nurturing Campaign Formula

Depending on which talking head you listen to, you're going to hear that it will take a minimum of seven impressions for somebody to buy something from you or become a warm prospect for you. The good news is that when you use ActionBrand Marketing, those seven impressions don't need to be seven individual advertisements that cost you several thousands of dollars each.

Instead, when you capture a prospect's contact information the first time with one ad, you can automatically show up with a "nurturing campaign" for as many impressions as you want for free or for pennies depending on your email provider or media method. For example, if you're using emails, you can bring those emails to life by embedding video content and links to a video series. Make yourself a list utilizing the formula revealed in "The 5 Branding Trust Triggers" chapter. Deliver consistent, useful, and interesting content, and include a call to action with each message sent. Your offers, at a minimum, can be the offer to speak with you to get specific answers to problems like a consultation. Always make it easy to take action.

The beauty of these "touches by email" is that they don't all need to be read to be effective. The mere fact that you show up in your prospect's inbox puts you in their mind, even if they overlook your updates and don't open your emails. When your list updates appear in their inboxes, this still counts as an impression.

Depending on the temperature of that prospect, you never know when they will become "in heat" for what it is that you do. They might have opted into your list with a feeble interest, but the temperature of their interest might go from cool to hot depending on what's going on in their life. When you keep showing up in their inbox, you can be top of mind when that temperature changes for them.

If You Sell the Invisible

Education-based marketing is vital if you offer a solution to a complicated problem or something that requires explaining. Suppose you sell the invisible, like insurance or consulting, or even something as mundane as wedding DJ entertainment. In that case, it is easy to create fascination in the market because a DJ is a significant consideration for someone preparing for a wedding.

It could be the first time they're planning a wedding, and their mind is racing and open to all the different facets of it. These facets may cause confusion, anxiety, or just curiosity. You can tap into this fascination with your education-based marketing content. Have fun creating content. Make sure you are ticking boxes that you know are already curiosities in your prospect's mind. Next, surprise them with content they didn't even realize they needed; open their eyes.

If You Sell a Tangible

Let's say you sell a car, for example. Do the prospects interested in buying a particular car model want more or less information? This leads us to the topic of "length of copy" or words.

You may often hear from family or friends: "That advertisement is way too long. Nobody is going to read something that long." Although they are well-meaning, they may be inexperienced, especially if they are not even interested in the advertised product, which leads them to give you bad advice unintentionally.

If you were speaking to interested parties, they likely would respond differently. They would say: "Oh my gosh! I've been looking for this. I'm going to read every single word." Think about what it is that these interested persons would want to know. Don't listen to well-meaning advice from novices if they're not likely buyers of that particular product. Their opinions are vague and not steeped in principle.

For example, if you're in the market for the newest electric car, would it be enough to get you to buy it if I send you a 4 x 6 postcard with a picture and a tagline that says, "It's sexy time!"?

Not likely! You probably want to know everything about this car because it's a considerable investment.

On the other hand, if I was selling you a steak and you're a vegetarian, you wouldn't care less if I sent you a single photograph on a postcard or a 20-page letter. Both marketing materials are going straight into the garbage.

Here's the lesson: **Write for buyers, not non-buyers.** You're trying not to offend a non-buyer who wouldn't give you a dime anyway by writing nothing. As a result, you are trading off real buyers because you didn't give them enough to entice their engagement and get them to want more.

As far as the length of the copy goes, I have an expression that may come off as a bit sexist, so I apologize in advance but take it in the fun spirit in which it was intended. "Copy is like a woman's skirt. It should be long enough to cover the important bits but short enough to get us excited and keep our attention." In other words, use as many words as you need to express the greater benefits of your product or service, but don't oversell it. Don't waste words but don't save words either.

The rule of thumb is you can write as much copy as you need to until it gets boring. This applies to video content as well. People interested in buying will absorb and soak up every word as long as it is fun, engaging, and fresh information that does not bore them.

These are the essential elements of an ActionBrand Marketing Funnel. Marketing should be simple. Once you've learned ActionBrand Marketing, your marketing will become instinctual. You'll gain the confidence to launch any business in the future, knowing that you could whip up the minimum effective dose ActionBrand Marketing campaigns to gain clients and customers fast while anchoring your brand in the minds of your prospects for accelerated acceptance and growth over time.

KEY TAKEAWAYS

➤ Always incorporate your ActionBrand DNA in every piece of marketing content you produce.

➤ Craft your Irresistible Offer so it stands out from your competitors.

➤ Simplify your lead generation page by focusing only on one problem, one free offer, and one call to action.

➤ Engineer your main website to convincingly display your wide range of offers besides the specific one that got your prospect to buy from you in the first place. Make sure you create an impression of value across all your offerings from your primary site.

➤ Pay close attention to the content updates you send to your mailing list subscribers. Craft specific strategies to change their buying temperature from cold to warm depending on whether you sell intangibles or tangibles.

"FREE" Organic Traffic vs Paid Advertising with Perry Marshall

> "Influencer marketing can be effective, but it's like solar power. It's not on-demand and you can't turn it up with a dial. Paid traffic is like electrical power from a utility company: You can get as much as you want, as long as you can pay for it."
>
> PERRY MARSHALL, AUTHOR OF ULTIMATE GUIDE TO GOOGLE ADS, 80/20 SALES & MARKETING, EVOLUTION 2.0

Mark's note to the reader: This book's intended scope is crafting an ActionBrand, including the strategy behind direct response marketing. Naturally, once you create your message and brand strategy, your next question is, "How do I get this message in front of the right audience?" The answer is to drive traffic from where your ideal audience hangs out.

Before the internet, the only way you could get a message to your audience, besides pinning flyers on cork boards in your community, would be paid advertising in newspapers, magazines, TV, radio, direct mail, or door hangers. It is shocking to think back at how limited the options were!

The internet brought about a new frontier and the deceptive belief that advertising can ultimately be free.

The topic of traffic is vast, the media choices are everchanging, and there are other books covering trending media channels. For *this* book, I want to memorialize a foundational principle that will remain evergreen. No matter what new channel, media, or app may pop up in the future, you can run it through this principle filter.

To address the topic of traffic, whether free or paid, I asked my esteemed colleague Perry Marshall to share an important insight. He literally "wrote the books" on traffic that I highly recommend you read *(Ultimate Guide to Google Ads, 80/20 Sales & Marketing, The Definitive Guide to YouTube Ads,* and *The Definitive Guide to TikTok Advertising).* There is nobody better to school you on this principle. - Mark Imperial

The "Free Model" vs. "Make $1 Model" by Perry Marshall

The rise of YouTube celebs (especially with them getting a share of ad revenue) has created a hysteria around social media influencers that have inspired thousands of aspiring stars and starlets to try as hard as humanly possible to "go viral."

They desire to become the next Gary Vaynerchuk / Hank Green / Laura Izumikawa / Joe Rogan / Addison Rae / Jordan Peterson / Tess Holiday / Vsauce / Vitus "V" Spehar / Emma Chamberlain / Abigail Behar / Humans Of New York. They post, comment, like, tweet, blog, and V-blog 24/7, hoping the algorithmic gods will smile upon them.

They record videos everywhere they walk and drive. They opine about everything under the sun, hoping that just one of those videos will get a million views.

This method works for a vanishingly small number of the people who try it. I believe it requires a certain indefinable "magic" or "star power" to work. I do not think it is at all honest to advertise this as a system that works reliably for anybody and everybody.

The greatest deception of the Free Model is the notion that it's "free." It's only free if you consider weeks, months, and years of your blood, sweat, and life (and your absence from the lives of your friends and family members) to be "free."

Oh yeah… and just because they're internet-famous doesn't guarantee they're rolling in dough. Very few internet celebs are actually "rich."

There is another method that is much more reliable, often over-looked, and far more formulaic and predictable. I call it the "Make $1 Model." It's where 80% of the wealth resides. And it's far more consistent and reliable than the free model.

The Make $1 Model says:

Test...

- Ads
- Landing Pages
- Offers

With **small advertising dollars** and **small quantities of time** until you **make one dollar**. What does "make one dollar" mean?

It means:

Spend $10 and make $11. Spend $100 and make $101. Spend $1000 and make $1001.

In other words, *just run the machine and tinker with it until it's in the black.* You don't worry about your labor. You can fix that later... for now, you just need to generate media exposure without losing money. Once you solve that problem, the rest is pretty straightforward. The hard part is over, and you can scale up.

How do you run the machine?

You test ads until you get a good Click Thru Rate. You test videos until you get a high completion rate.

You test landing pages until you get a good signup rate. You test offers until you find one that sells well.

This is incomparably easier than trying to become the next Joe Rogan. And you can literally do this with lunch money if you don't have a lot of cash. **Most entrepreneurs I know - thousands of people who make six and seven-figure incomes and many companies that have been sold for millions and tens of millions of dollars - built their businesses THIS way.**

Software companies, manufacturing firms, subscription services, consultants and coaches, dentists and cosmetic surgeons, delivery services, real estate investors, sellers of nutritional supplements, and household goods.

"Make \$1" is the 21st-century version of what Claude Hopkins was teaching in his classic book "Scientific Advertising" written in 1918. This is eminently reliable.

It's almost inevitable that by the time you've tested 30 ads, 10 landing pages, and five offers, you'll have a sales machine that nets you a positive return.

How Much Should You Spend to Acquire a Customer?

There's a really simple way to answer this question, which is great for beginners... then, once you have your sea legs, the answer changes a bit.

The simple answer is: If you can invest $100 in advertising and product costs and sell your product for $101 and literally "make one dollar," then you are over the hump.

If you're new, hang on to this and run with it until you make one dollar.

If you can acquire a customer at break-even or better, then as soon as you sell them anything else, you're profitable. This invokes...

The Magic Gumball Machine Question:

If you had a magic gumball machine so
that when you put money in,
out comes a new customer, what's the
most you'd be willing to put in?

This is an incredibly powerful question. First, most people don't know the answer. Second, it reduces customer acquisition to dollars and cents, which is the goal of all advertising. Third, it naturally invites you to consider the Lifetime Value of a customer instead of only the first sale.

For a brand new advertising medium with cheap click prices, early in the game, advertisers will be able to make a profit by acquiring a new customer the very first time. But that doesn't last very long. Soon, the world figures it out, and prices go up.

So again, for beginning advertisers, your goal is to "make one dollar."

For more advanced advertisers, the real question is: How far negative are you willing to go to acquire your customer? If your margin on a product is $30, can you afford to spend $35? $40? $50?

The thing that makes you able to "go deep" is your ability to generate repeat sales. If your first sale is $50 and you're able to spend $100 to acquire that $50 customer because you know that in 3-6 months, you'll get all that money back and more, you become a formidable player in the ad marketplace.

I've got a story for ya...

A few weeks ago, there was a knock on the door. My 11-year-old daughter answered. It was the dad of two of her friends. They lived across the street from our house for several years. She still sees them from time to time.

The dad asked for me, but I wasn't available. The next day, he texted.

"I've got a good friend who follows your work. She runs a non-profit. Could we stop by and ask you a few questions?"

Since our kids are friends, I said yes. Turns out his friend performs a very particular kind of therapy. She gets exceptional results for her clients. She began peppering me with questions, which were all over the place, and vibed mostly with the "Free Model."

After digging for a while, I discovered that she had at one time successfully sold an expensive "48-hour immersion experience" where clients make great progress in a very short period of time.

I told her:

Just sell THAT. Do not pass go, do not collect $200, do not blink or even think until you have figured out how to run an ad, build a list, and sell seats to your workshop. Don't worry about whether you make a profit on the first workshop. Just make ONE dollar.

A week later, she sent a thank you note solemnly pledging to do precisely that.

Thus, her journey began.

Selling the ActionBrand Way

Marketing is everything you do to get a potential customer interested in your business, and selling is all about convincing that potential customer to say yes to your offer.

Now, selling isn't really what we're digging into in this book, but it's crucial to understand how your ActionBrand Marketing strategy sets the stage for that sales conversation. Your messaging should do most of the selling beforehand, ensuring that when a customer steps into a meeting with you, they're already on board.

Your carefully constructed sequence of ActionBrand Marketing messages and the thoughtfully prepared materials should have done their magic already, positioning you as the obvious choice. If you've played your cards right, they've picked you just by scheduling the appointment. It's your job now to reassure them they're making an intelligent choice and present an offer they can't refuse.

See, most people's marketing and selling strategies focus on impressing their industry peers, which is pointless for the prospect. We're going to delve more into this trap in a later section.

There's no one-size-fits-all approach to this, but in this chapter, I will walk you through the method I swear by - a game-changer I like to call "The 3 D Killer One Call Close."

The 3 D Killer One Call Close

I first shared this technique with my DJ entertainer marketing and sales students, so remember to think outside the box when applying it to your business. I dubbed it the "One Call Close" because selling a DJ entertainment package - whether for a wedding, bar mitzvah, or corporate event - comes with various options, making it a tricky sell. But I'll show you how to shift your presentation style. The key is simplicity because a confused mind tends to be indecisive. If your business offers a complex package that needs a thorough explanation, chances are you're making it too hard for your customers to decide.

Now let's look at it from a different angle.

The traditional way DJ companies used to sell their services was flawed. They'd brag about their expertise and throw three or four packages at the couple. And then the add-ons came in - cocktail hour music, lighting, photo booths, you name it. With all these options, it's like diving headfirst into Pandora's box of indecision. This selling style only prolongs the sales cycle, leaving the DJ to chase and follow up, which most would agree isn't their strong suit.

But the 3 D Killer One Call Close method? It eliminates the chase, wrapping up the deal in the first call. This method is consultative in nature. It's not about bragging about your company and its achievements. Sure, you can sprinkle those facts in, but most of that info should have been shared before this sales appointment.

The focus of the consultation is to tune into your prospect's dreams and the conversation in their mind, which they will practically tell you. The 3 Ds in the name stand for **D**angers, **D**reams, and **D**ependables.

Set the Tone

The conversation starts with a simple question to set the mood. I'd ask a bride or a couple: "Imagine we're chatting a few months after your big day. Looking back, what would need to have happened for you to feel satisfied with how everything went?" You're asking them to define success in their terms. Plus, you're planting yourself in their future successful scenario.

This question usually sparks a lively discussion, often leading the couple to ponder and share what success looks like to them, sometimes for the first time. And trust me, it's an enjoyable conversation to have!

Dangers

First up is Dangers. Here, I probe the couple about their concerns: "What are you most worried about for your reception? Anything specific you'd like to avoid? Any potential pitfalls we should be aware of?"

Like other aspects of ActionBrand Marketing, this is the dash of salt in the cookie dough - a little bit of contrast to keep them mindful of the stakes at hand. There is no need to linger too long on this part; a brief discussion is enough.

In the context of DJ entertainment, most couples worry about people not dancing. This presents a perfect opportunity to discuss music, ask about the guests' backgrounds, and assure them that you'll cater to different musical tastes, even taking song requests from guests. A pinch of salt is all it takes.

Dreams

Then we move on to Dreams. I ask the couple: "If you could wave a magic wand and make your wedding exactly how you want it, what would it look like? What's your dream scenario?"

Notice how this question encourages them to imagine their dream wedding- a super fun party or a classy event. Sometimes, I might ask: "If you had to describe your dream wedding in three words, what would they be?"

Their answers give you an insight into their vision and priorities, allowing you to align your services with their dream. For instance, if they say "elegant," you can show them photos of classy lighting setups. If they say "fun," you can discuss fun elements like dance contests.

Dependables

Finally, we have Dependables. This is where you encourage your prospect to think about what they can count on, like who's going to be the life of the party. A question like "Who among your guests can we rely on? Who's going to be tearing up the dance floor all night?" always brings smiles and laughter as the couple pictures their friends, family, or coworkers. You want your customers to feel confident in their ability to succeed, linking that feeling subconsciously to you since you guide them through this conversation.

What I've found is that this method has two killer benefits:

- It builds trust in you as you guide them through envisioning their dream wedding.
- It boosts their self-belief and belief in their event's success.

This is often overlooked: not only should your customers trust you and your services, but they also need to trust in themselves and their capabilities. They need to believe that they can make it happen.

The Offer

Once you've navigated the terrain of the 3 D conversation, the next step is to present your proposal. Remember, our objective is the One Call Close. We don't want to leave things up in the air. When the proposal is crafted accurately, following up becomes unnecessary.

Let's go back to my DJ entertainer scenario. After hearing my clients out, I'd usually offer them a vision of an unforgettable evening that checks all their boxes: their favorite music, activities they enjoy, and spotlighting the people they mentioned. Then, I'd inform them, "We offer various packages priced according to the custom program we design for you."

Here's the crux of it all. I'd assert: "Choosing a package is crucial, but it's not something you need to decide right now. You've got ample time to mull it over." The element of scarcity is brought into play here. In the DJ context, the scarcity is their event date and the fact that I only have one booking slot available for that day. Surprisingly, it often slips people's minds that their desired service provider might already be booked.

Then, I'd steer the conversation towards: "The only choice you need to make at this moment is whether you think we're the right fit."

To simplify the decision-making process, I'd assure them: "We make it straightforward with a minimal deposit to reserve your date. This ensures that nobody else can snap us up." Then, I'd collect either $500 or $1000, which is, of course, credited toward the final package they opt for, which they only have to worry about a month before their date.

This line of questioning significantly reduces the pressure linked to the sale. It eliminates all the discourse and ambiguity about which package the couple prefers. Following a traditional presentation, the couple typically wants to regroup and spend hours discussing it. This is counterproductive for a DJ sale.

My strategy removes that option to retreat and merely asks them to decide if they want to work with me. I conducted a comprehensive two-hour training on this method, and what I've shared here is just a nutshell version.

Can you see how having your prospect make a simple rather than complicated decision can immediately get you that sale?

I also include a no-strings-attached, seven-day right of first refusal guarantee to eliminate any apprehension about the offer. Within seven days, if they find someone they believe is a better fit, they can call and won't be charged a dime. In fact, their credit card is only charged after those seven days.

I've discovered that once people agree to the deposit, they like to tick it off their list because they have numerous other tasks to deal with. I haven't lost a sale due to that seven-day guarantee.

By this point, they've already decided they're comfortable with me. The couple doesn't need to converse about that aspect. They want to deliberate over the minutiae of the package. I don't need to be part of that dialogue. That discussion can be conducted on another day, which I term "the final arrangements." This subsequent call also serves as an opportunity to upsell packages.

You may have noticed that the essence of ActionBrand Marketing is to understand what your customer values the most and deliver it to them. It's not about singing your own praises, bragging about your credentials, years in business, or anything else. All of that is taken care of in advance, subtly woven into our ActionBrand Marketing messages that lead up to the sales meeting.

KEY TAKEAWAYS

> "Pre-sell" your clients with materials that display your expertise. This could be a book or interview article introducing your company, its accomplishments, credentials, and experience.

> The sales call is for sealing the deal, given that the prospect has "self-selected" by arranging the call.

> Employing the 3 D Killer One Call Close system allows the prospect to sell themselves on your offering by aligning your proposition with their desired outcomes.

The Nucleus of Your Marketing: A Signature Book

Having your own published book is a secret sauce for boosting your business or personal brand. Nothing can build credibility as effectively as showcasing your expertise - a crucial advantage in today's trust-focused economy.

Your Book Helps People Understand You Fast

Folks are inundated with marketing noise all day, and their schedules are more hectic than ever. They're on the lookout for shortcuts - they don't have time to dig deep into what you're all about.

Here's where your book steps in, acting as that much-needed short-cut, helping people grasp quickly who you are and what you do. Craft a catchy title, and you'll inspire their dreams and ambitions. Not only that, but your book will also clarify who you assist and how.

If you're a self-employed professional or business owner, prioritiz-ing creating your signature book is a must.

Memorialize Your Methods and Brand in Your Target Customer's Mind

Just a glance at your book's cover and title, and people will get your vibe. Your book is a fantastic tool to imprint your values in the minds of your prospects.

Why not name your unique methods? Doing so makes your ap-proach appear proprietary, unique, and, well, it is!

Consider Tony Robbins. Without his book "Personal Power" and the related training system and course under the Personal Power® brand, he might have been just another run-of-the-mill self-development guru. That book, my first purchase from him, skyrocketed his career and solidified him as the Personal Power® guy in everyone's mind.

You can do the same - brand your system, and give it a purpose. No matter if Tony is hosting Fiji retreats or offering personalized coaching, when you hear his name, you think Personal Power®.

Feeling like you don't do anything exceptional? Like you're a carbon copy of everyone else in your field because you all graduated from the same school? Not so fast!

You are unique. You bring your own background, influences, beliefs, and mentors to the table. Throughout your journey, you've developed unique hacks, tips, tricks, and insights. The best thing you can do for others and yourself is to give your unique methods a memorable name and offer it to the world as your exclusive solution in the field.

The Two Types of Books You Need to Create Right Away

Type I: Signature Book

As discussed in this chapter, this book embodies your system, your method. The title of your signature book will become your identifier for years to come. It lays the groundwork for the brand you want to be synonymous with, becoming a bookmark in people's minds. When asked what you do, you could hand over an autographed copy of your book while you excuse yourself for a bathroom break. By the time you're back, if they need your services, you're set for a riveting conversation.

The Birth of "The Value Journey" Brand Name: A Story of Brand Transformation Using a Signature Book

Branding plays a pivotal role in distinguishing one company from another. Behind every compelling brand name is often a story, a catalyst that sets the course of a transformation.

One of my clients was an exit planner with a company named "Journey Consulting." The founder, a passionate advisor with a unique system under her wing, had been using a relatively common term for her system: "Exit Planning." While descriptive, it lacked the uniqueness and memorability a brand-centric approach could offer.

As we discussed her company and services, I thought, "Why not leverage the strength and imagery of her company's name, 'Journey Consulting,' and combine it with the ultimate outcome she provides to her clients?" After all, her approach was all about guiding businesses through a transformative journey, culminating in them realizing their enterprise's true value.

With this perspective, I suggested a rebranding of her system that would encapsulate both the essence of her company's name and the result she aimed for her clients to achieve. Thus, "The Value Journey" was conceived, and it became her brand *and* the title of her signature book. With the book as a tangible manifestation of her proprietary system, it served a dual purpose. Not only was it an informative guide, but it also became a tool to memorialize her brand in the minds of her clients. And with the strategic implementation of ActionBrand Marketing campaigns, "The Value Journey" was not just seared into the memories of her clients but imprinted onto the collective consciousness of her entire target market.

Type 2: Anthology Book

Next up is the anthology book, a fast track to authorship. Here, you contribute one chapter to a book with a specific theme alongside several other authors.

Imagine a book called "Real Estate Insights" where agents nationwide comment on the post-pandemic market. Each agent contributes one interview, and voila! The book will be ready in weeks. Upon release, all the agents become published authors on Amazon, in full view of the world.

This route gives you quick authorship (a great first step while you're still working on your signature book) and provides third-party credibility. Being included in the book implies the publisher considers you as a leading expert in the field, signaling to your prospects that other authorities recognize your expertise.

At the bare minimum, aim to have both of these types of books in your portfolio. I can't emphasize enough your book's crucial role in your ActionBrand Marketing journey. That's why I wrote **"Books Grow Business,"** an entire book dedicated to guiding you through crafting your own signature book.

Whether you're a DIY enthusiast or a busy bee who needs a professional writer to translate your ideas into a compelling narrative, I've got you covered. Even if you're tight on time, a few short hours with our writing team over the phone can transform your thoughts into an authentic book; even your mom would believe you wrote it!

Grab a copy at BooksGrowBusiness.com and kickstart the growth of your business today!

Putting It All Together

Now that you've learned all the essential elements of ActionBrand Marketing, it all comes down to implementation to get results. Although no two businesses are alike, this chapter will lay out the minimum effective dose of an implementation plan that puts ActionBrand Marketing into your business and profits into your bank account.

Your Results Are Linked to the Degree to Which You Implement

Let's take it from the top as if you're ActionBrand Marketing a new business or rebranding your existing business. Here are the seven steps to implement ActionBrand Marketing.

Step 1: Start With the End Goal in Mind

What is your primary objective for this branding or rebranding of your company? Are you looking for clearer messaging? Are you looking for superb client acquisition? Start with your goals.

If client acquisition is your goal, one of the best places to start is by asking, "What is your most popular service or product?" In other words, what is the front door for your business? What do you believe your ideal customer or client needs first?

Refer to the chapter "The DNA of an ActionBrand" to help you determine your target audience and brainstorm on your own or with your team about what the target audience wants. What are the biggest problems that you help them overcome? And what do you help them achieve, or what transformation do you help them accomplish?

Step 2: ActionBrand DNA Message — Internal and External

While referring back to "The DNA of an ActionBrand" chapter, consider those two internal and external messages. The internal message is just a clear, defining statement that you and your company will follow to guide the direction of your messaging.

The external message is the cleaned-up version, which sounds normal when you say it and does not sound robotic or contrived. It's a message that is conversational in tone and one that you can speak at a cocktail party.

Here is an example: "Many business owners and executives know they need to publish a book but don't have the time or talent to write or don't know where to start. Our professional writing team turns their knowledge into a book using their voice in about a month that is so good their own mothers would believe they wrote it."

This should be an all-encompassing statement about your company or ActionBrand that you can place everywhere on your marketing assets, including your business card, the signature line of an email, or at the top of your website. It is the message that you want the public, especially your raving fans, to be able to memorize and repeat.

Step 3: Create Your Lead Magnet

This should be a specific offer or family of offers that bring people to your front door. You will use it to build your list and generate leads.

Remember, a signature book is one of my favorite ActionBrand Marketing assets to use as a lead magnet. It can also be a special report, a video series, a webinar, or a checklist. Another favorite of mine is a free service or product offer. What can you afford to give away that leads to sales? What is something of value that people will gladly exchange their contact information for?

Remember the example I gave of an event photographer offering to take your picture for free and delivering the watermarked photos? He followed up by asking if you would like to buy the full-resolution versions for print or on T-shirts, mugs, scrapbooks, or other merchandise.

Step 4: Create Your ActionBrand Web Properties

Work with your graphic designer and website programmers to develop your landing pages and core website. From the previous step, determine your lead magnets and craft individual, standalone landing pages for each offer.

When you drive people from very specific ads and offers to a landing page that matches, they know that they are in the right place, and there is only one thing for them to do: exchange their contact information for your offer.

We create these landing pages to keep the visitor from doing anything else except deciding on your offer. Sending them straight to your core website can end up confusing your prospects. Only show them your core website after you've collected their contact information. Your core website can serve as the hub for your individual offers.

Step 5: Determine Your Traffic Sources

Where does your target audience hang out? How can you reach them most efficiently? Could you run lead-generation ads in specialized media? You will send your offers to this audience, so you'll want to know exactly where they spend their time.

One of the greatest gifts to business owners is that audiences have been diversified by so many different media that you can now reach them affordably if you take the time to identify these publications.

For example, when I ran my DJ business and wanted wedding clients, instead of advertising in a national magazine, which would have wasted a lot of money considering I only needed clients in Chicagoland, I found "Chicago Wedding Magazine." As a special added bonus, this magazine also gave me a monthly list of sub-scribers. I did two things from this list called "farming."

Firstly, I placed a lead-generating ad in the magazine that offered my book on "Remarkable Wedding Receptions." The second thing I did was mail a postcard or a sales letter offering the same book to the monthly list I received. I got a small number of responses from the list, but those responses told me very specifically that they were planning their wedding reception and needed reception entertainment.

Rather than wasting money and resources by mailing everyone on that list a copy of my book, I would only send it to those who responded. There will inevitably be a percentage of subscribers on that list each month who already have their entertainment and would not need the book. That's why I call this "farming." My method enabled me to spend much more on an impressive package sent to the smaller list of respondents.

Be sure to use this tactic anywhere you need your more extensive list to be broken down to determine and identify ideal prospects and separate them from folks who likely do not need your service. You do this by carefully crafting your offer.

Step 6: Create Your ActionBrand Nurture Campaign

A "nurture campaign" involves automated scheduled messages that enable your brand to stay in touch with your list members.

Your campaign helps your business stay in front of your prospect. This way, you are always top of mind when they are ready to purchase. You need to run a nurture campaign because people aren't necessarily ready to buy your main offer the day that they request your information.

Now that you know your likely future buyers, you want to keep showing up so that you're there when they are ready to purchase. But this begs the question: "How frequently should you be showing up in their inbox?"

There's no hard and fast rule. The only rule you should follow is to avoid becoming boring or an annoying pest. In other words, if you're always offering something new, of value, or interest while remaining entertaining and fun, your prospect will be happy to receive a message from you daily. You've probably heard that people need to hear a message seven or eight times before they're ready to purchase. This is the principle behind your nurture campaign.

Typically, the first email sent out delivers the lead magnet promise. Why? The first email is likely going to the person who entered their information on your landing page to join your list.

For instance, if the promise of that offer is a special report, the first email should deliver that report along with a soft offer of some related value. If you're a wedding DJ promising a special report on "How to Have the Most Unforgettable and Fun Wedding

Reception Ever," you would deliver it whether it's a 38-video series or a PDF.

At the bottom of the email, you can offer a complimentary consultation and give it an ActionBrand name. Let's say, "A Dream Reception Entertainment Plan." Send them an offer to "The Dream Reception Entertainment Plan" with a link to your calendar.

For example, my free offer in my book publishing business is a digital copy of my book, which I accompany with a complimentary signature book discovery session. The prospect can claim the discovery session by booking a time on my calendar.

After this point, you can start sending topical emails delivered on a pre-set schedule after that primary first email. I recommend a minimum of a weekly topic email. However, you can increase that by emailing every two or three days. To create this message series, you can use ideas from "The ActionBrand Marketing Assets" and "ActionBrand Trust Triggers" chapters.

For a quick and dirty shortcut, I can give you the formula to create your first 20 email messages:

Take out a piece of paper and write down the ten most frequently asked questions about the problem you help your clients solve. Next, on that same sheet of paper, write down ten "should ask questions." This exercise sets up your FAQ and SAQ.

A "should ask question" is something very eye-opening that your target audience should be asking but perhaps don't know enough about the subject to ask. These are often revelatory and demonstrate your expertise, so much so that you gain credibility and authority.

These twenty individual messages can be delivered in an email by PDF or plain text. Or you can try my favorite method, a video series. Video adds an extra touch and personalizes your marketing message by showcasing your personality and expertise.

Remember, each email message context should end with a similar offer to your consultation.

ActionBrand Offer Wheel

Up to this point, we've discussed how nurturing emails deliver helpful information and aim to solve your target audience's problems. Mixed in with these messages should be deliberate promotional emails that make a direct offer. If these are date-related events, they don't have to be automated. You can simply broadcast them at specific times of the year. Or, if it's something evergreen, you can include them in the nurturing campaign sequence schedule.

Let's say you're a coach or consultant that teaches specialized knowledge for a particular industry, like professional speakers.

The first step is to write down an inventory of the core competencies you teach. Perhaps these can be:

1. How to craft a signature speech.
2. How to present on webinars and teleseminars.
3. How to develop coaching programs like "train the trainer" programs.
4. How to host your own events.

If these are your core areas of coaching, put them on a calendar wheel. You can run four promotions per year, 90 days apart.

With the example above, organize your coaching topic categories in logical order. What is the front door? What is the first investment that makes the most sense for your customers to make with you? What will they get from that investment? What transformation will they experience from it? Is there a logical next step that will take them to the next phase in your ActionBrand Offer Wheel?

Don't be shy! You can make specific offers to your list every once in a while as long as you're not doing it so much that your list subscribers see you as a pitchman.

Step 7: ActionBrand Tribe Nurturing

This is the branding element of ActionBrand Marketing. This step involves speaking to your raving fans and communicating to the audience you have gathered.

What assets can you give the fans that will bring them closer to you and let them spread your name as a by-product of being a raving fan? At the end of the day, people want to belong. People express themselves through their connections.

For example, people wear logos that they relate to. They like letting the brand story express their identity simply by wearing the apparel. Work with your graphic designers to create the ideal expression of your brand and assets you can give to the raving fans that help them spread the word for you. One of the greatest things you can give your tribe is extra copies of your signature book. Alternatively, you can distribute VIP coupons to your list members to give away. Each coupon entitles the receiver to a copy of your book.

You can apply this minimum effective dose to launch or relaunch any business or brand. There are hundreds of ways to be right; some are more effective and efficient than others. To figure these out, you must test.

Once you embrace ActionBrand Marketing, you may discover that your nurture campaign is the most fun part of your business. Remember that this is the money-getting part of your business because nothing else matters, not even the CEO's job until somebody buys something.

Advanced: Profit Loops

Once you've embraced ActionBrand Marketing, you can develop campaigns for the five areas in your business that bring you money. I call these areas "profit loops." They are profit loops because the messaging is very specific to each area of focus.

I'll be covering these areas in more detail in a forthcoming book. However, here's a brief overview of "The Five Profit Loops." The five loops are 1) Lead Generation Loop, 2) Conversion Loop, 3) Value Ascension Loop, 4) Retention Frequency Loop, and 5) Referral Loop.

Most businesses incur huge waste by focusing only on new customers. You can get more results from the same money, time, and energy you spend marketing your business. When you discover the five profit loops, you'll understand how 40% up to 400% increases can be easily attained.

The Lead Generation Loop

This loop is about generating new prospects and turning cold traffic into warm. It all starts with your ideal prospect matched to the ideal message. If we double the number of quality leads you receive each week, and everything else stays the same, you double your business.

Conversion Loop

People buy from those they trust. This is where you build your prospects' trust faster. This loop involves the messaging campaign that you create and all the value that you deliver to those new prospects that came in from your lead generation loop.

Value Ascension Loop

This is where you focus on maximizing the value of your new customer or client. Focus on finding ways to increase their average value to you, whether it's by creating upsell offers or simply increasing fees. This is also where you cross-sell to the other areas of your Offer Wheel.

Retention Frequency Loop

There is real money in retention. According to Forbes Magazine, a mere 5% increase in retention can result in a 75% increase in profit. The Harvard Business Review also stated that new customer acquisition is anywhere from 5x to 25x more expensive than retaining an existing one. This is a brutal blast of reality that you shouldn't just be thinking about new customers but focusing on keeping the ones you already have.

This loop should include more ActionBranding and Tribe Nurturing. It should also include the building of a community.

Features like membership levels or special community events are terrific in this loop.

Referral Loop

The second easiest sale you'll ever make is to someone referred to you. You can make this automatic. When you work on your Referral Loop, you can quickly increase the number of "I got a guy" referrals you get.

A customer newsletter is one of the primary tools to use and deploy in the Referral Loop. Newsletters are a perfect way to stay in touch to acknowledge your clients or customers of the month and to offer gifts that your recipients can give to friends and family to get them on your list.

Have you ever heard the expression, "Work *on* your business, not *in* it?" This is what it means to work on your business. You should be working on optimizing these five key areas in your business. You don't have to tackle it all at once. However, a steady focus on sharpening all areas has a compounding, exponential effect on your profitability.

Having a fine-tuned system is an asset that will impact your bottom line and add a tangible marketing asset that will count in the increase of your company's valuation. People value predictable systems, not just random acts of marketing.

KEY TAKEAWAYS

> ‣ Start implementing ActionBrand Marketing by focusing on the outcome you wish to achieve.

> ‣ Be clear about your ActionBrand DNA statement and consistently apply it, whether external or internal.

> ‣ Create your lead magnet and offer it as a premium in exchange for prospects joining your mailing list.

> ‣ Nurture your community, fanbase, or tribe with helpful scheduled email updates mixed with time-specific announcements. All communications must reflect the value in your brand so you stay top of mind.

Epilogue

"Great Marketing and Branding Make the Buyer
Feel Empowered, Confident, and Smart."

- MARK IMPERIAL

Congratulations! By reaching the end of this book, you have now armed yourself with a robust blueprint for crafting an ActionBrand Marketing Action Plan tailored to your business. Few books can offer such a comprehensive snapshot of a powerful strategy designed to bolster your brand and boost your revenue simultaneously.

Welcome to the ActionBrand Marketing methodology. You have become part of an elite group of high-achievers, no longer prone to the pitfalls of "awareness-only," resource-draining advertising tactics. From this point forward, each campaign you develop promises a quantifiable return on investment, a process you can continually refine and perfect.

The insights you've gained equip you to revolutionize your business and aid other entrepreneurs in harnessing this potent system for their enterprises.

Regrettably, too much capital gets unwittingly squandered because business owners consider marketing and branding an afterthought. It's disheartening to see a business's most effective campaign being its "Going Out of Business" sale, a move that shatters dreams and wreaks havoc on families. This is a reality I aspire to prevent, serving as the driving force behind this book.

If your ambitions reach beyond personal success and towards aiding other business owners, consider taking a step further to become certified in the ActionBrand Marketing framework. Such certification will allow you to dive deeper, master, and utilize your newfound skills to assist other business owners while retaining all the proceeds. We at ActionBrand Marketing never deduct a royalty from our Advisors. For more information, visit **www. actionbrandmarketing.com**.

Embark on your journey, strive for greatness, and aim to enrich the lives of others tenfold to a hundredfold compared to what you receive. This is the essence of ethically profiting wildly - not only will you enhance your business, but you'll also contribute positively to the world at large!

Ready to master ActionBrand Marketing
for your business or as a coach?

Go beyond "This is ActionBrand Marketing"
and join our mastery programs, attend our
retreats and intensives, or become a certified
coach. Transform your skills and impact.

Start now at **www.ActionBrandMarketing.com**
Your marketing revolution awaits!

About the Author

Mark Imperial is a distinguished best-selling author. He had the honor of training in direct response marketing under the renowned Dan S. Kennedy, becoming one of his select few Certified Independent Business Advisors. Mark led Dan Kennedy's Chicago SW Mastermind Group for eight years and wrote the "Grow Your Local Business" monthly column in the No BS Marketing Letter, guiding tens of thousands of business owners.

Mark gained his branding skills while being the experiential marketing implementer for globally loved brands, including Nintendo™, Pokémon™, and Under Armour™.

Through his firsthand experiences with the powers of direct response marketing and strategic branding, Mark blended these practices into one unified approach - ActionBrand Marketing.

Mark currently resides in the western suburbs of Chicago with his beloved Shannon, his bonus kids Max and Felix, a turtle, a bearded dragon, and Fortune the French Bulldog. For more information, visit www.markimperial.com and www.ActionBrandMarketing.com.

Made in the USA
Monee, IL
24 May 2024

58691208R00115